Daily

Sage

Intake

"You are the light of the world"

Pastor Steve Lawes
Vineyard Community Church
Big Pine Key, Florida

Daily Sage Intake
Pastor Steve Lawes
Vineyard Community Church
100 County Rd
Big Pine Key, FL 33043
www.spiritualfervor.com

Every known copyrighted source that has been used has been duly credited.

The Proverbs themselves are from the Jesus Moment Bible. The Jesus Moment Bible is a devotional Bible that I am editing from the well-respected ASV Bible which is in the public domain. For a complete discussion on the Jesus Moment Bible and the ASV Bible please go to www.jesusmomentbible.com.

ISBN 978-0-9890473-2-6   3rd Printing October, 2014

Special Thanks

To Alice, my love, you are a constant reminder to me of the favor of the Lord! (Proverbs 18:22)

To my children, Sarah and Douglas, and to their spouses Paul and Kimberly, you are a source of delight to me! (Proverbs 23:24)

To my grand-children, Sam, Avery, Stevie, Ellie and the one on the way, you are my crown! (Proverbs 17:6)

To my mom, Sylvia, thank you for being my mom! (Proverbs 31:8)

To Barry, Fran, Georgina, Billy, Angie and Scott; what an awesome group of Pastors to labor in His vineyard with!

To Charlie, Tommy, and Garrett; thank you for your amazing support!

To the awesome Vineyard community: What a joy it is to serve with you in the Florida Keys. Thank you for your constant support and encouragement in allowing me to try new things as we press on together in our mission of "One More".

Table of Contents

Introduction

The **Daily Sage Intake** is the second book in a series of devotionals for disciples. The first book in the series, **Daily Psalt Intake**, was developed from the merging of what I believe are two important concepts of the now and forever life in Christ. The first concept comes from the prominence of the Psalms in the daily spiritual disciplines of the early church. The second concept comes from Matthew 5:13 where Jesus tells His followers that they are the 'salt of the earth'.

In much the same way that the Psalms help us develop and season (psalt) our prayer lives, the Proverbs help to develop the way that we live out our life "in Christ" in a fallen world on a broken planet. The Proverbs give us wisdom and guidance as we try to live by doing the next right thing and help us to be "the light of the world". The **Daily Sage Intake** includes a morning and evening reading of the Proverbs which will have you reading all 31 Proverbs, twice each month. Combined with the **Daily Psalt Intake** readings this will provide a strong foundation for your devotional life.

By keeping ourselves spiritually healthy and alive in a consistent devotional life incorporating a regular reading and praying through of the Proverbs and the Psalter, we will be able to fulfill our calling to have an impact on the world around us, to be the light of the world and the (p)salt of the earth! With that said, let me encourage you to "Psalt and Sage Daily"!

*Note: The Proverbs are usually short but rather intense sentences. They are sometimes arranged so that two sentences kind of illustrate each other. At other times they appear sort of randomly. In the **Daily Sage** Intake I did not attempt to group the sentences but let them stand verse by verse so that you can pray about how they fit or don't fit together. What they all do, however, is to point out good and evil, giving us wisdom and helping us to live by choosing to do the next right thing!*

Daily Sage Intake

Welcome to a devotional journey that is designed to help you develop healthy spiritual disciplines to keep your spiritual fervor. The journey (which began with the **Daily Psalt Intake**) continues with a reading from the Proverbs every morning and evening, so that you read the entire book of Proverbs twice each month. The Proverbs give practical suggestions for everyday living. The Proverbs are not just a collection of interesting tidbits; they are a call to action. I have added little comments on each of the Proverbs that appear at the beginning of each reading. If you find them distracting, just skip over them. The important thing is to get in the habit of reading your **Daily Sage Intake** every morning and evening. The daily readings should only take about five minutes every morning and another five minutes every evening. I would also encourage you to get in the habit of reading the Proverbs out loud. This will help you stay more engaged with the Proverbs as you read them. Don't worry about the readings that are left over on the months with less than 31 days since you will be reading them often throughout the course of the year.

Day 1 – Morning Sage Intake

The Proverbs help prepare us to live as "the light of the world". They are filled with "Sage" advice and wisdom about how to live in relationship with God and others. They give us practical advice on how to live by trying to do the next right thing.

Proverbs 1

1 The proverbs of Solomon, the son of David, king of Israel:

2 to know wisdom and instruction; to discern the words of understanding;

3 to receive instruction in wise dealing, in righteousness, justice, and equity;

4 to give prudence to the simple, knowledge and discretion to the young man:

5 that the wise man may hear, and increase in learning; that the man of understanding may attain to sound counsel:

6 to understand a proverb, and parables, the words and riddles of the wise.

7 The fear of the LORD is the beginning of knowledge; but the foolish despise wisdom and instruction.

8 My son, listen to your father's instruction, and don't forsake your mother's teaching:

9 for they will be a garland to grace your head, and chains around your neck.

10 My son, if sinners entice you, don't consent.

11 If they say, "Come with us, Let's lay in wait for blood; let's lurk secretly for the innocent without cause;

12 let's swallow them up alive like Sheol, and whole, like those who go down into the pit.

13 We'll find all valuable wealth. We'll fill our houses with plunder.

14 You shall cast your lot amongst us. We'll all have one purse."

15 My son, don't walk on the path with them. Keep your foot from their path,

16 for their feet run to evil. They hurry to shed blood.

17 For in vain is the net spread in the sight of any bird:

18 but these lay wait for their own blood. They lurk secretly for their

own lives.

19 So are the ways of everyone who is greedy for gain. It takes away the life of its owners.

20 Wisdom calls aloud in the street. She utters her voice in the public squares.

21 She calls at the head of noisy places. At the entrance of the city gates, she utters her words:

22 "How long, you simple ones, will you love simplicity? How long will mockers delight themselves in mockery, and fools hate knowledge?

23 Turn at my reproof. Behold, I will pour out my spirit on you. I will make known my words to you.

24 Because I have called, and you have refused; I have stretched out my hand, and no one has paid attention;

25 but you have ignored all my counsel, and wanted none of my reproof;

26 I also will laugh at your disaster. I will mock when calamity overtakes you;

27 when calamity overtakes you like a storm, when your disaster comes on like a whirlwind; when distress and anguish come on you.

28 Then will they call on me, but I will not answer. They will seek me diligently, but they will not find me;

29 because they hated knowledge, and didn't choose the fear of the LORD.

30 They wanted none of my counsel. They despised all my reproof.

31 Therefore they will eat of the fruit of their own way, and be filled with their own schemes.

32 For the backsliding of the simple will kill them. The careless ease of fools will destroy them.

33 But whoever listens to me will dwell securely, and will be at ease, without fear of harm."

"You are the light of the world" Sage Daily!

Day 1 – Evening Sage Intake

Proverbs 2 encourages us to seek God's wisdom like we were searching for silver or hidden treasure!

Proverbs 2

1 My son, if you will receive my words, and store up my commandments within you;
2 So as to turn your ear to wisdom, and apply your heart to understanding;
3 Yes, if you call out for discernment, and lift up your voice for understanding;
4 If you seek her as silver, and search for her as for hidden treasures:
5 then you will understand the fear of the LORD, and find the knowledge of God.
6 For the LORD gives wisdom. Out of his mouth comes knowledge and understanding.
7 He lays up sound wisdom for the upright. He is a shield to those who walk in integrity;
8 that he may guard the paths of justice, and preserve the way of his saints.
9 Then you will understand righteousness and justice, equity and every good path.
10 For wisdom will enter into your heart. Knowledge will be pleasant to your soul.
11 Discretion will watch over you. Understanding will keep you,
12 to deliver you from the way of evil, from the men who speak perverse things;
13 who forsake the paths of uprightness, to walk in the ways of darkness;
14 who rejoice to do evil, and delight in the perverseness of evil;
15 who are crooked in their ways, and wayward in their paths:
16 To deliver you from the strange woman, even from the foreigner who flatters with her words;
17 who forsakes the friend of her youth, and forgets the covenant of her God:
18 for her house leads down to death, her paths to the departed spirits.

19 None who go to her return again, neither do they attain to the paths of life:

20 that you may walk in the way of good men, and keep the paths of the righteous.

21 For the upright will dwell in the land. The perfect will remain in it.

22 But the wicked will be cut off from the land. The treacherous will be rooted out of it.

Day 2 – Morning Sage Intake

Proverbs 3 is one of my favorites. It is filled with encouragement to experience now and forever life in His story as we live by trying to do the next right thing!

Proverbs 3

1 My son, don't forget my teaching; but let your heart keep my commandments:

2 for length of days, and years of life, and peace, will they add to you.

3 Don't let kindness and truth forsake you. Bind them around your neck. Write them on the tablet of your heart.

4 So you will find favor and good understanding in the sight of God and man.

5 Trust in the LORD with all your heart, and don't lean on your own understanding.

6 In all your ways acknowledge him, and he will make your paths straight.

7 Don't be wise in your own eyes. Fear the LORD, and depart from evil.

8 It will be health to your body, and nourishment to your bones.

9 Honor the LORD with your substance, with the first fruits of all your increase:

10 so your barns will be filled with plenty, and your vats will overflow with new wine.

11 My son, don't despise the LORD's discipline, neither be weary of his reproof:

12 for whom the LORD loves, he reproves; even as a father reproves the son in whom he delights.

13 Happy is the man who finds wisdom, the man who gets understanding.

14 For her good profit is better than getting silver, and her return is better than fine gold.

15 She is more precious than rubies. None of the things you can desire are to be compared to her.

16 Length of days is in her right hand. In her left hand are riches and honor.

17 Her ways are ways of pleasantness. All her paths are peace.

18 She is a tree of life to those who lay hold of her. Happy is everyone who retains her.

19 By wisdom the LORD founded the earth. By understanding, he established the heavens.

20 By his knowledge, the depths were broken up, and the skies drop down the dew.

21 My son, let them not depart from your eyes. Keep sound wisdom and discretion:

22 so they will be life to your soul, and grace for your neck.

23 Then you shall walk in your way securely. Your foot won't stumble.

24 When you lie down, you will not be afraid. Yes, you will lie down, and your sleep will be sweet.

25 Don't be afraid of sudden fear, neither of the desolation of the wicked, when it comes:

26 for the LORD will be your confidence, and will keep your foot from being taken.

27 Don't withhold good from those to whom it is due, when it is in the power of your hand to do it.

28 Don't say to your neighbor, "Go, and come again; tomorrow I will give it to you," when you have it by you.

29 Don't devise evil against your neighbor, since he dwells securely by you.

30 Don't strive with a man without cause, if he has done you no harm.

31 Don't envy the man of violence. Choose none of his ways.

32 For the perverse is an abomination to the LORD, but his friendship is with the upright.

33 The LORD's curse is in the house of the wicked, but he blesses the habitation of the righteous.

34 Surely he mocks the mockers, but he gives grace to the humble.

35 The wise will inherit glory, but shame will be the promotion of fools.

Day 2 – Evening Sage Intake

To make sure we are paying attention, Solomon uses this chapter to review the main points he has shared in the previous three chapters.

Proverbs 4

1 Listen, sons, to a father's instruction. Pay attention and know understanding;
2 for I give you sound learning. Don't forsake my law.
3 For I was a son to my father, tender and an only child in the sight of my mother.
4 He taught me, and said to me: "Let your heart retain my words. Keep my commandments, and live.
5 Get wisdom. Get understanding. Don't forget, neither swerve from the words of my mouth.
6 Don't forsake her, and she will preserve you. Love her, and she will keep you.
7 Wisdom is supreme. Get wisdom. Yes, though it costs all your possessions, get understanding.
8 Esteem her, and she will exalt you. She will bring you to honor, when you embrace her.
9 She will give to your head a garland of grace. She will deliver a crown of splendor to you."
10 Listen, my son, and receive my sayings. The years of your life will be many.
11 I have taught you in the way of wisdom. I have led you in straight paths.
12 When you go, your steps will not be hampered. When you run, you will not stumble.
13 Take firm hold of instruction. Don't let her go. Keep her, for she is your life.
14 Don't enter into the path of the wicked. Don't walk in the way of evil men.
15 Avoid it, and don't pass by it. Turn from it, and pass on.

16 For they don't sleep, unless they do evil. Their sleep is taken away, unless they make someone fall.

17 For they eat the bread of wickedness, and drink the wine of violence.

18 But the path of the righteous is like the dawning light that shines more and more until the perfect day.

19 The way of the wicked is like darkness. They don't know what they stumble over.

20 My son, attend to my words. Turn your ear to my sayings.

21 Let them not depart from your eyes. Keep them in the center of your heart.

22 For they are life to those who find them, and health to their whole body.

23 Keep your heart with all diligence, for out of it is the wellspring of life.

24 Put away from yourself a perverse mouth. Put corrupt lips far from you.

25 Let your eyes look straight ahead. Fix your gaze directly before you.

26 Make the path of your feet level. Let all of your ways be established.

27 Don't turn to the right hand nor to the left. Remove your foot from evil.

Day 3 – Morning Sage Intake

Try and live this day by remembering that God is always watching. Living this way will help to make us people of integrity; not constantly changing to match the crowd or the circumstance, just being who we are at all times in the Lord.

Proverbs 5

1 My son, pay attention to my wisdom. Turn your ear to my understanding:

2 that you may maintain discretion, that your lips may preserve knowledge.

3 For the lips of an adulteress drip honey. Her mouth is smoother than

oil,

4 but in the end she is as bitter as wormwood, and as sharp as a two-edged sword.

5 Her feet go down to death. Her steps lead straight to Sheol.

6 She gives no thought to the way of life. Her ways are crooked, and she doesn't know it.

7 Now therefore, my sons, listen to me. Don't depart from the words of my mouth.

8 Remove your way far from her. Don't come near the door of her house,

9 lest you give your honor to others, and your years to the cruel one;

10 lest strangers feast on your wealth, and your labors enrich another man's house.

11 You will groan at your latter end, when your flesh and your body are consumed,

12 and say, "How I have hated instruction, and my heart despised reproof;

13 neither have I obeyed the voice of my teachers, nor turned my ear to those who instructed me!

14 I have come to the brink of utter ruin, amongst the gathered assembly."

15 Drink water out of your own cistern, running water out of your own well.

16 Should your springs overflow in the streets, streams of water in the public squares?

17 Let them be for yourself alone, not for strangers with you.

18 Let your spring be blessed. Rejoice in the wife of your youth.

19 A loving doe and a graceful deer—let her breasts satisfy you at all times. Be captivated always with her love.

20 For why should you, my son, be captivated with an adulteress? Why embrace the bosom of another?

21 For the ways of man are before the LORD's eyes. He examines all his paths.

22 The evil deeds of the wicked ensnare him. The cords of his sin hold him firmly.

23 He will die for lack of instruction. In the greatness of his folly, he will go astray.

Day 3 – Evening Sage Intake

Reading, studying, memorizing, and meditating on the Word of God is one of the most important spiritual disciplines that you can develop in order to experience now and forever life in His story. Make it your daily practice to get your Daily Psalt Intake, your Daily Sage Intake, and your Daily Bread Intake!

Proverbs 6

1 My son, if you have become collateral for your neighbor, if you have struck your hands in pledge for a stranger;

2 You are trapped by the words of your mouth. You are ensnared with the words of your mouth.

3 Do this now, my son, and deliver yourself, since you have come into the hand of your neighbor. Go, humble yourself. Press your plea with your neighbor.

4 Give no sleep to your eyes, nor slumber to your eyelids.

5 Free yourself, like a gazelle from the hand of the hunter, like a bird from the snare of the fowler.

6 Go to the ant, you sluggard. Consider her ways, and be wise;

7 which having no chief, overseer, or ruler,

8 provides her bread in the summer, and gathers her food in the harvest.

9 How long will you sleep, sluggard? When will you arise out of your sleep?

10 A little sleep, a little slumber, a little folding of the hands to sleep:

11 so your poverty will come as a robber, and your scarcity as an armed man.

12 A worthless person, a man of iniquity, is he who walks with a perverse mouth;

13 who winks with his eyes, who signals with his feet, who motions with his fingers;

14 in whose heart is perverseness, who devises evil continually, who always sows discord.

15 Therefore his calamity will come suddenly. He will be broken suddenly, and that without remedy.

16 There are six things which the LORD hates; yes, seven which are

an abomination to him:

17 haughty eyes, a lying tongue, hands that shed innocent blood;

18 a heart that devises wicked schemes, feet that are swift in running to mischief,

19 a false witness who utters lies, and he who sows discord amongst brothers.

20 My son, keep your father's commandment, and don't forsake your mother's teaching.

21 Bind them continually on your heart. Tie them around your neck.

22 When you walk, it will lead you. When you sleep, it will watch over you. When you awake, it will talk with you.

23 For the commandment is a lamp, and the law is light. Reproofs of instruction are the way of life,

24 to keep you from the immoral woman, from the flattery of the wayward wife's tongue.

25 Don't lust after her beauty in your heart, neither let her captivate you with her eyelids.

26 For a prostitute reduces you to a piece of bread. The adulteress hunts for your precious life.

27 Can a man scoop fire into his lap, and his clothes not be burnt?

28 Or can one walk on hot coals, and his feet not be scorched?

29 So is he who goes in to his neighbor's wife. Whoever touches her will not be unpunished.

30 Men don't despise a thief, if he steals to satisfy himself when he is hungry:

31 but if he is found, he shall restore seven times. He shall give all the wealth of his house.

32 He who commits adultery with a woman is void of understanding. He who does it destroys his own soul.

33 He will get wounds and dishonor. His reproach will not be wiped away.

34 For jealousy arouses the fury of the husband. He won't spare in the day of vengeance.

35 He won't regard any ransom, neither will he rest content, though you give many gifts.

Day 4 – Morning Sage Intake

The enemy constantly uses the same three tricks to try and distract you from the life that God has created you for. The three tricks are; the lust of the flesh, the lust of the eyes, and the pride of life. Stay focused on Jesus as you walk through the day, and the enemies tricks will not succeed in distracting you.

Proverbs 7

1 My son, keep my words. Lay up my commandments within you.
2 Keep my commandments and live! Guard my teaching as the apple of your eye.
3 Bind them on your fingers. Write them on the tablet of your heart.
4 Tell wisdom, "You are my sister." Call understanding your relative,
5 that they may keep you from the strange woman, from the foreigner who flatters with her words.
6 For at the window of my house, I looked out through my lattice.
7 I saw amongst the simple ones. I discerned amongst the youths a young man void of understanding,
8 passing through the street near her corner, he went the way to her house,
9 in the twilight, in the evening of the day, in the middle of the night and in the darkness.
10 Behold, there a woman met him with the attire of a prostitute, and with crafty intent.
11 She is loud and defiant. Her feet don't stay in her house.
12 Now she is in the streets, now in the squares, and lurking at every corner.
13 So she caught him, and kissed him. With an impudent face she said to him:
14 "Sacrifices of peace offerings are with me. Today I have paid my vows.
15 Therefore I came out to meet you, to diligently seek your face, and I have found you.
16 I have spread my couch with carpets of tapestry, with striped cloths of the yarn of Egypt.
17 I have perfumed my bed with myrrh, aloes, and cinnamon.

18 Come, let's take our fill of loving until the morning. Let's solace ourselves with loving.

19 For my husband isn't at home. He has gone on a long journey.

20 He has taken a bag of money with him. He will come home at the full moon."

21 With persuasive words, she led him astray. With the flattering of her lips, she seduced him.

22 He followed her immediately, as an ox goes to the slaughter, as a fool stepping into a noose.

23 Until an arrow strikes through his liver, as a bird hurries to the snare, and doesn't know that it will cost his life.

24 Now therefore, sons, listen to me. Pay attention to the words of my mouth.

25 Don't let your heart turn to her ways. Don't go astray in her paths,

26 for she has thrown down many wounded. Yes, all her slain are a mighty army.

27 Her house is the way to Sheol, going down to the rooms of death.

Day 4 – Evening Sage Intake

John 14:6-7 – Jesus said to him, "I am the way, the truth, and the life. No one comes to the Father, except through me. If you had known me, you would have known my Father also. From now on, you know him, and have seen him."

Proverbs 8

1 Doesn't wisdom cry out? Doesn't understanding raise her voice?

2 On the top of high places by the way, where the paths meet, she stands.

3 Beside the gates, at the entry of the city, at the entry doors, she cries aloud:

4 "To you men, I call! I send my voice to the sons of mankind.

5 You simple, understand prudence. You fools, be of an understanding heart.

6 Hear, for I will speak excellent things. The opening of my lips is for right things.

7 For my mouth speaks truth. Wickedness is an abomination to my

lips.

8 All the words of my mouth are in righteousness. There is nothing crooked or perverse in them.

9 They are all plain to him who understands, right to those who find knowledge.

10 Receive my instruction rather than silver; knowledge rather than choice gold.

11 For wisdom is better than rubies. All the things that may be desired can't be compared to it.

12 "I, wisdom, have made prudence my dwelling. Find out knowledge and discretion.

13 The fear of the LORD is to hate evil. I hate pride, arrogance, the evil way, and the perverse mouth.

14 Counsel and sound knowledge are mine. I have understanding and power.

15 By me kings reign, and princes decree justice.

16 By me princes rule; nobles, and all the righteous rulers of the earth.

17 I love those who love me. Those who seek me diligently will find me.

18 With me are riches, honor, enduring wealth, and prosperity.

19 My fruit is better than gold, yes, than fine gold; my yield than choice silver.

20 I walk in the way of righteousness, in the middle of the paths of justice;

21 That I may give wealth to those who love me. I fill their treasuries.

22 "The LORD possessed me in the beginning of his work, before his deeds of old.

23 I was set up from everlasting, from the beginning, before the earth existed.

24 When there were no depths, I was born, when there were no springs abounding with water.

25 Before the mountains were settled in place, before the hills, I was born;

26 while as yet he had not made the earth, nor the fields, nor the beginning of the dust of the world.

27 When he established the heavens, I was there; when he set a circle on the surface of the deep,

28 when he established the clouds above, when the springs of the deep became strong,

29 when he gave to the sea its boundary, that the waters should not violate his commandment, when he marked out the foundations of the earth;

30 then I was the craftsman by his side. I was a delight day by day, always rejoicing before him,

31 Rejoicing in his whole world. My delight was with the sons of men.

32 "Now therefore, my sons, listen to me, for blessed are those who keep my ways.

33 Hear instruction, and be wise. Don't refuse it.

34 Blessed is the man who hears me, watching daily at my gates, waiting at my door posts.

35 For whoever finds me, finds life, and will obtain favor from the LORD.

36 But he who sins against me wrongs his own soul. All those who hate me love death."

Day 5 – Morning Sage Intake

Joshua 24:15b – ...choose today whom you will serve; whether the gods which your fathers served that were beyond the River, or the gods of the Amorites, in whose land you dwell; but as for me and my house, we will serve the LORD.

Proverbs 9

1 Wisdom has built her house. She has carved out her seven pillars.

2 She has prepared her meat. She has mixed her wine. She has also set her table.

3 She has sent out her maidens. She cries from the highest places of the city:

4 "Whoever is simple, let him turn in here!" As for him who is void of understanding, she says to him,

5 "Come, eat some of my bread, drink some of the wine which I have mixed!

6 Leave your simple ways, and live. Walk in the way of understanding."

7 He who corrects a mocker invites insult. He who reproves a wicked

man invites abuse.

8 Don't reprove a scoffer, lest he hate you. Reprove a wise man, and he will love you.

9 Instruct a wise man, and he will be still wiser. Teach a righteous man, and he will increase in learning.

10 The fear of the LORD is the beginning of wisdom. The knowledge of the Holy One is understanding.

11 For by me your days will be multiplied. The years of your life will be increased.

12 If you are wise, you are wise for yourself. If you mock, you alone will bear it.

13 The foolish woman is loud, undisciplined, and knows nothing.

14 She sits at the door of her house, on a seat in the high places of the city,

15 to call to those who pass by, who go straight on their ways,

16 "Whoever is simple, let him turn in here." as for him who is void of understanding, she says to him,

17 "Stolen water is sweet. Food eaten in secret is pleasant."

18 But he doesn't know that the departed spirits are there, that her guests are in the depths of Sheol.

Day 5 – Evening Sage Intake

The first nine chapters of the Proverbs serve as an introduction or preface to the Proverbs. Here in Chapter 10 they begin in earnest. They are usually short but rather intense sentences. They are sometimes arranged so that two sentences kind of illustrate each other. At other times they appear sort of randomly. In the Daily Sage Intake I did not attempt to group the sentences but let them stand verse by verse so that you can pray about how they fit or don't fit together. What they all do, however, is to point out good and evil, giving us wisdom and helping us to live by choosing to do the next right thing!

Proverbs 10

1 The proverbs of Solomon. A wise son makes a glad father; but a foolish son brings grief to his mother.

2 Treasures of wickedness profit nothing, but righteousness delivers from death.

3 The LORD will not allow the soul of the righteous to go hungry, but he thrusts away the desire of the wicked.

4 He becomes poor who works with a lazy hand, but the hand of the diligent brings wealth.

5 He who gathers in summer is a wise son, but he who sleeps during the harvest is a son who causes shame.

6 Blessings are on the head of the righteous, but violence covers the mouth of the wicked.

7 The memory of the righteous is blessed, but the name of the wicked will rot.

8 The wise in heart accept commandments, but a chattering fool will fall.

9 He who walks blamelessly walks surely, but he who perverts his ways will be found out.

10 One winking with the eye causes sorrow, but a chattering fool will fall.

11 The mouth of the righteous is a spring of life, but violence covers the mouth of the wicked.

12 Hatred stirs up strife, but love covers all wrongs.

13 Wisdom is found on the lips of him who has discernment, but a rod is for the back of him who is void of understanding.

14 Wise men lay up knowledge, but the mouth of the foolish is near ruin.

15 The rich man's wealth is his strong city. The destruction of the poor is their poverty.

16 The labor of the righteous leads to life. The increase of the wicked leads to sin.

17 He is in the way of life who heeds correction, but he who forsakes reproof leads others astray.

18 He who hides hatred has lying lips. He who utters a slander is a fool.

19 In the multitude of words there is no lack of disobedience, but he who restrains his lips does wisely.

20 The tongue of the righteous is like choice silver. The heart of the wicked is of little worth.

21 The lips of the righteous feed many, but the foolish die for lack of understanding.

22 The LORD's blessing brings wealth, and he adds no trouble to it.

23 It is a fool's pleasure to do wickedness, but wisdom is a man of understanding's pleasure.

24 What the wicked fear, will overtake them, but the desire of the righteous will be granted.

25 When the whirlwind passes, the wicked is no more; but the righteous stand firm forever.

26 As vinegar to the teeth, and as smoke to the eyes, so is the sluggard to those who send him.

27 The fear of the LORD prolongs days, but the years of the wicked shall be shortened.

28 The prospect of the righteous is joy, but the hope of the wicked will perish.

29 The way of the LORD is a stronghold to the upright, but it is a destruction to the workers of iniquity.

30 The righteous will never be removed, but the wicked will not dwell in the land.

31 The mouth of the righteous produces wisdom, but the perverse tongue will be cut off.

32 The lips of the righteous know what is acceptable, but the mouth of the wicked is perverse.

Day 6 – Morning Sage Intake

Proverbs 11 contains some weighty sayings!

Proverbs 11

1 A false balance is an abomination to the LORD, but accurate weights are his delight.

2 When pride comes, then comes shame, but with humility comes wisdom.

3 The integrity of the upright shall guide them, but the perverseness of the treacherous shall destroy them.

4 Riches don't profit in the day of wrath, but righteousness delivers from death.

5 The righteousness of the blameless will direct his way, but the wicked shall fall by his own wickedness.

6 The righteousness of the upright shall deliver them, but the unfaithful will be trapped by evil desires.

7 When a wicked man dies, hope perishes, and expectation of power comes to nothing.

8 A righteous person is delivered out of trouble, and the wicked takes his place.

9 With his mouth the godless man destroys his neighbor, but the righteous will be delivered through knowledge.

10 When it goes well with the righteous, the city rejoices. When the wicked perish, there is shouting.

11 By the blessing of the upright, the city is exalted, but it is overthrown by the mouth of the wicked.

12 One who despises his neighbor is void of wisdom, but a man of understanding holds his peace.

13 One who brings gossip betrays a confidence, but one who is of a trustworthy spirit is one who keeps a secret.

14 Where there is no wise guidance, the nation falls, but in the multitude of counselors there is victory.

15 He who is collateral for a stranger will suffer for it, but he who refuses pledges of collateral is secure.

16 A gracious woman obtains honor, but violent men obtain riches.

17 The merciful man does good to his own soul, but he who is cruel troubles his own flesh.

18 Wicked people earn deceitful wages, but one who sows righteousness reaps a sure reward.

19 He who is truly righteous gets life. He who pursues evil gets death.

20 Those who are perverse in heart are an abomination to the LORD, but those whose ways are blameless are his delight.

21 Most certainly, the evil man will not be unpunished, but the offspring of the righteous will be delivered.

22 Like a gold ring in a pig's snout, is a beautiful woman who lacks discretion.

23 The desire of the righteous is only good. The expectation of the wicked is wrath.

24 There is one who scatters, and increases yet more. There is one who withholds more than is appropriate, but gains poverty.

25 The liberal soul shall be made fat. He who waters shall be watered also himself.

26 People curse someone who withholds grain, but blessing will be on

the head of him who sells it.

27 He who diligently seeks good seeks favor, but he who searches after evil, it shall come to him.

28 He who trusts in his riches will fall, but the righteous shall flourish as the green leaf.

29 He who troubles his own house shall inherit the wind. The foolish shall be servant to the wise of heart.

30 The fruit of the righteous is a tree of life. He who is wise wins souls.

31 Behold, the righteous shall be repaid in the earth; how much more the wicked and the sinner!

Day 6 – Evening Sage Intake

The first verse of Proverbs 12 is one of my favorites. "Whoever loves correction loves knowledge, but he who hates reproof is stupid." Solomon just telling it like it is!

Proverbs 12

1 Whoever loves correction loves knowledge, but he who hates reproof is stupid.

2 A good man shall obtain favor from the LORD, but he will condemn a man of wicked devices.

3 A man shall not be established by wickedness, but the root of the righteous shall not be moved.

4 A worthy woman is the crown of her husband, but a disgraceful wife is as rottenness in his bones.

5 The thoughts of the righteous are just, but the advice of the wicked is deceitful.

6 The words of the wicked are about lying in wait for blood, but the speech of the upright rescues them.

7 The wicked are overthrown, and are no more, but the house of the righteous shall stand.

8 A man shall be commended according to his wisdom, but he who has a warped mind shall be despised.

9 Better is he who is lightly esteemed, and has a servant, than he who honors himself, and lacks bread.

10 A righteous man respects the life of his animal, but the tender mercies of the wicked are cruel.

11 He who tills his land shall have plenty of bread, but he who chases fantasies is void of understanding.

12 The wicked desires the plunder of evil men, but the root of the righteous flourishes.

13 An evil man is trapped by sinfulness of lips, but the righteous shall come out of trouble.

14 A man shall be satisfied with good by the fruit of his mouth. The work of a man's hands shall be rewarded to him.

15 The way of a fool is right in his own eyes, but he who is wise listens to counsel.

16 A fool shows his annoyance the same day, but one who overlooks an insult is prudent.

17 He who is truthful testifies honestly, but a false witness lies.

18 There is one who speaks rashly like the piercing of a sword, but the tongue of the wise heals.

19 Truth's lips will be established forever, but a lying tongue is only momentary.

20 Deceit is in the heart of those who plot evil, but joy comes to the promoters of peace.

21 No mischief shall happen to the righteous, but the wicked shall be filled with evil.

22 Lying lips are an abomination to the LORD, but those who do the truth are his delight.

23 A prudent man keeps his knowledge, but the hearts of fools proclaim foolishness.

24 The hands of the diligent ones shall rule, but laziness ends in slave labor.

25 Anxiety in a man's heart weighs it down, but a kind word makes it glad.

26 A righteous person is cautious in friendship, but the way of the wicked leads them astray.

27 The slothful man doesn't roast his game, but the possessions of diligent men are prized.

28 In the way of righteousness is life; in its path there is no death.

Day 7 – Morning Sage Intake

Ephesians 4:29 – Let no corrupt speech proceed out of your mouth, but only what is good for building others up as the need may be, that it may give grace to those who hear.

Proverbs 13

1 A wise son listens to his father's instruction, but a scoffer doesn't listen to rebuke.
2 By the fruit of his lips, a man enjoys good things; but the unfaithful crave violence.
3 He who guards his mouth guards his soul. One who opens wide his lips comes to ruin.
4 The soul of the sluggard desires, and has nothing, but the desire of the diligent shall be fully satisfied.
5 A righteous man hates lies, but a wicked man brings shame and disgrace.
6 Righteousness guards the way of integrity, but wickedness overthrows the sinner.
7 There are some who pretend to be rich, yet have nothing. There are some who pretend to be poor, yet have great wealth.
8 The ransom of a man's life is his riches, but the poor hear no threats.
9 The light of the righteous shines brightly, but the lamp of the wicked is snuffed out.
10 Pride only breeds quarrels, but with ones who take advice is wisdom.
11 Wealth gained dishonestly dwindles away, but he who gathers by hand makes it grow.
12 Hope deferred makes the heart sick, but when longing is fulfilled, it is a tree of life.
13 Whoever despises instruction will pay for it, but he who respects a command will be rewarded.
14 The teaching of the wise is a spring of life, to turn from the snares of death.
15 Good understanding wins favor; but the way of the unfaithful is hard.

16 Every prudent man acts from knowledge, but a fool exposes folly.
17 A wicked messenger falls into trouble, but a trustworthy envoy gains healing.
18 Poverty and shame come to him who refuses discipline, but he who heeds correction shall be honored.
19 Longing fulfilled is sweet to the soul, but fools detest turning from evil.
20 One who walks with wise men grows wise, but a companion of fools suffers harm.
21 Misfortune pursues sinners, but prosperity rewards the righteous.
22 A good man leaves an inheritance to his children's children, but the wealth of the sinner is stored for the righteous.
23 An abundance of food is in poor people's fields, but injustice sweeps it away.
24 One who spares the rod hates his son, but one who loves him is careful to discipline him.
25 The righteous one eats to the satisfying of his soul, but the belly of the wicked goes hungry.

Day 7 – Evening Sage Intake

If you don't have any oxen in the stable, then you don't have to shovel manure. However, you also don't have all the benefits that come from the work of the oxen. Real life includes moving into situations we would often rather not deal with, but it is in facing up to the difficult things that we most often experience the grace and mercy of the Lord. So, pick up your shovels and be thankful for the oxen!

Proverbs 14

1 Every wise woman builds her house, but the foolish one tears it down with her own hands.
2 He who walks in his uprightness fears the LORD, but he who is perverse in his ways despises him.
3 The fool's talk brings a rod to his back, but the lips of the wise protect them.
4 Where no oxen are, the crib is clean, but much increase is by the strength of the ox.

5 A truthful witness will not lie, but a false witness pours out lies.
6 A scoffer seeks wisdom, and doesn't find it, but knowledge comes easily to a discerning person.
7 Stay away from a foolish man, for you won't find knowledge on his lips.
8 The wisdom of the prudent is to think about his way, but the folly of fools is deceit.
9 Fools mock at making atonement for sins, but amongst the upright there is good will.
10 The heart knows its own bitterness and joy; he will not share these with a stranger.
11 The house of the wicked will be overthrown, but the tent of the upright will flourish.
12 There is a way which seems right to a man, but in the end it leads to death.
13 Even in laughter the heart may be sorrowful, and mirth may end in heaviness.
14 The unfaithful will be repaid for his own ways; likewise a good man will be rewarded for his ways.
15 A simple man believes everything, but the prudent man carefully considers his ways.
16 A wise man fears, and shuns evil, but the fool is hot headed and reckless.
17 He who is quick to become angry will commit folly, and a crafty man is hated.
18 The simple inherit folly, but the prudent are crowned with knowledge.
19 The evil bow down before the good, and the wicked at the gates of the righteous.
20 The poor person is shunned even by his own neighbor, but the rich person has many friends.
21 He who despises his neighbor sins, but blessed is he who has pity on the poor.
22 Don't they go astray who plot evil? But love and faithfulness belong to those who plan good.
23 In all hard work there is profit, but the talk of the lips leads only to poverty.
24 The crown of the wise is their riches, but the folly of fools crowns them with folly.

25 A truthful witness saves souls, but a false witness is deceitful.

26 In the fear of the LORD is a secure fortress, and he will be a refuge for his children.

27 The fear of the LORD is a fountain of life, turning people from the snares of death.

28 In the multitude of people is the king's glory, but in the lack of people is the destruction of the prince.

29 He who is slow to anger has great understanding, but he who has a quick temper displays folly.

30 The life of the body is a heart at peace, but envy rots the bones.

31 He who oppresses the poor shows contempt for his Maker, but he who is kind to the needy honors him.

32 The wicked is brought down in his calamity, but in death, the righteous has a refuge.

33 Wisdom rests in the heart of one who has understanding, and is even made known in the inward part of fools.

34 Righteousness exalts a nation, but sin is a disgrace to any people.

35 The king's favor is towards a servant who deals wisely, but his wrath is towards one who causes shame.

Here at the end of the first week of the Daily Sage Intake, I want to encourage you to keep on making the reading of the Proverbs a priority in your life. If you keep it up for another couple of weeks, the regular daily reading of the Proverbs will become a lifelong habit like the one you developed with the Psalms in Daily Psalt Intake.

Day 8 – Morning Sage Intake

God is omniscient, omnipresent, and omnipotent. He is all knowing, ever present, and all powerful. Nothing is hidden from Him. Even though He is fully aware of all our brokenness, He loves us with an everlasting love that was displayed at the Cross!

Proverbs 15

1 A gentle answer turns away wrath, but a harsh word stirs up anger.
2 The tongue of the wise commends knowledge, but the mouth of fools gush out folly.
3 The LORD's eyes are everywhere, keeping watch on the evil and the good.
4 A gentle tongue is a tree of life, but deceit in it crushes the spirit.
5 A fool despises his father's correction, but he who heeds reproof shows prudence.
6 In the house of the righteous is much treasure, but the income of the wicked brings trouble.
7 The lips of the wise spread knowledge; not so with the heart of fools.
8 The sacrifice made by the wicked is an abomination to the LORD, but the prayer of the upright is his delight.
9 The way of the wicked is an abomination to the LORD, but he loves him who follows after righteousness.
10 There is stern discipline for one who forsakes the way: whoever hates reproof shall die.
11 Sheol and Abaddon are before the LORD—how much more then the hearts of the children of men!
12 A scoffer doesn't love to be reproved; he will not go to the wise.
13 A glad heart makes a cheerful face; but an aching heart breaks the spirit.
14 The heart of one who has understanding seeks knowledge, but the mouths of fools feed on folly.
15 All the days of the afflicted are wretched, but one who has a cheerful heart enjoys a continual feast.
16 Better is little, with the fear of the LORD, than great treasure with trouble.

17 Better is a dinner of herbs, where love is, than a fattened calf with hatred.

18 A wrathful man stirs up contention, but one who is slow to anger appeases strife.

19 The way of the sluggard is like a thorn patch, but the path of the upright is a highway.

20 A wise son makes a father glad, but a foolish man despises his mother.

21 Folly is joy to one who is void of wisdom, but a man of understanding keeps his way straight.

22 Where there is no counsel, plans fail; but in a multitude of counselors they are established.

23 Joy comes to a man with the reply of his mouth. How good is a word at the right time!

24 The path of life leads upward for the wise, to keep him from going downward to Sheol.

25 The LORD will uproot the house of the proud, but he will keep the widow's borders intact.

26 The LORD detests the thoughts of the wicked, but the thoughts of the pure are pleasing.

27 He who is greedy for gain troubles his own house, but he who hates bribes will live.

28 The heart of the righteous weighs answers, but the mouth of the wicked gushes out evil.

29 The LORD is far from the wicked, but he hears the prayer of the righteous.

30 The light of the eyes rejoices the heart. Good news gives health to the bones.

31 The ear that listens to reproof lives, and will be at home amongst the wise.

32 He who refuses correction despises his own soul, but he who listens to reproof gets understanding.

33 The fear of the LORD teaches wisdom. Before honor is humility.

Day 8 – Evening Sage Intake

James 4:6 – But he gives more grace. Therefore it says, "God resists the proud, but gives grace to the humble."

Proverbs 16

1 The plans of the heart belong to man, but the answer of the tongue is from the LORD.

2 All the ways of a man are clean in his own eyes; but the LORD weighs the motives.

3 Commit your deeds to the LORD, and your plans shall succeed.

4 The LORD has made everything for its own end—yes, even the wicked for the day of evil.

5 Everyone who is proud in heart is an abomination to the LORD: they shall certainly not be unpunished.

6 By mercy and truth iniquity is atoned for. By the fear of the LORD men depart from evil.

7 When a man's ways please the LORD, he makes even his enemies to be at peace with him.

8 Better is a little with righteousness, than great revenues with injustice.

9 A man's heart plans his course, but the LORD directs his steps.

10 Inspired judgements are on the lips of the king. He shall not betray his mouth.

11 Honest balances and scales are the LORD's; all the weights in the bag are his work.

12 It is an abomination for kings to do wrong, for the throne is established by righteousness.

13 Righteous lips are the delight of kings. They value one who speaks the truth.

14 The king's wrath is a messenger of death, but a wise man will pacify it.

15 In the light of the king's face is life. His favor is like a cloud of the spring rain.

16 How much better it is to get wisdom than gold! Yes, to get understanding is to be chosen rather than silver.

17 The highway of the upright is to depart from evil. He who keeps

his way preserves his soul.

18 Pride goes before destruction, and a haughty spirit before a fall.

19 It is better to be of a lowly spirit with the poor, than to divide the plunder with the proud.

20 He who heeds the Word finds prosperity. Whoever trusts in the LORD is blessed.

21 The wise in heart shall be called prudent. Pleasantness of the lips promotes instruction.

22 Understanding is a fountain of life to one who has it, but the punishment of fools is their folly.

23 The heart of the wise instructs his mouth, and adds learning to his lips.

24 Pleasant words are a honeycomb, sweet to the soul, and health to the bones.

25 There is a way which seems right to a man, but in the end it leads to death.

26 The appetite of the laboring man labors for him; for his mouth urges him on.

27 A worthless man devises mischief. His speech is like a scorching fire.

28 A perverse man stirs up strife. A whisperer separates close friends.

29 A man of violence entices his neighbor, and leads him in a way that is not good.

30 One who winks his eyes to plot perversities, one who compresses his lips, is bent on evil.

31 Grey hair is a crown of glory. It is attained by a life of righteousness.

32 One who is slow to anger is better than the mighty; one who rules his spirit, than he who takes a city.

33 The lot is cast into the lap, but its every decision is from the LORD.

You can always get your Daily Sage Intake on your computer, smart phone, or tablet at www.spiritualfervor.com!

Day 9 – Morning Sage Intake

I often think of verse 28 to try and help me keep from inserting my foot into my mouth. "Even a fool, when he keeps silent, is counted wise. When he shuts his lips, he is thought to be discerning."

Proverbs 17

1 Better is a dry morsel with quietness, than a house full of feasting with strife.
2 A servant who deals wisely will rule over a son who causes shame, and shall have a part in the inheritance amongst the brothers.
3 The refining pot is for silver, and the furnace for gold, but the LORD tests the hearts.
4 An evildoer heeds wicked lips. A liar gives ear to a mischievous tongue.
5 Whoever mocks the poor reproaches his Maker. He who is glad at calamity shall not be unpunished.
6 Children's children are the crown of old men; the glory of children are their parents.
7 Arrogant speech isn't fitting for a fool, much less do lying lips fit a prince.
8 A bribe is a precious stone in the eyes of him who gives it; wherever he turns, he prospers.
9 He who covers an offense promotes love; but he who repeats a matter separates best friends.
10 A rebuke enters deeper into one who has understanding than a hundred lashes into a fool.
11 An evil man seeks only rebellion; therefore a cruel messenger shall be sent against him.
12 Let a bear robbed of her cubs meet a man, rather than a fool in his folly.
13 Whoever rewards evil for good, evil shall not depart from his house.
14 The beginning of strife is like breaching a dam, therefore stop contention before quarreling breaks out.
15 He who justifies the wicked, and he who condemns the righteous, both of them alike are an abomination to the LORD.

16 Why is there money in the hand of a fool to buy wisdom, since he has no understanding?

17 A friend loves at all times; and a brother is born for adversity.

18 A man void of understanding strikes hands, and becomes collateral in the presence of his neighbor.

19 He who loves disobedience loves strife. One who builds a high gate seeks destruction.

20 One who has a perverse heart doesn't find prosperity, and one who has a deceitful tongue falls into trouble.

21 He who becomes the father of a fool grieves. The father of a fool has no joy.

22 A cheerful heart makes good medicine, but a crushed spirit dries up the bones.

23 A wicked man receives a bribe in secret, to pervert the ways of justice.

24 Wisdom is before the face of one who has understanding, but the eyes of a fool wander to the ends of the earth.

25 A foolish son brings grief to his father, and bitterness to her who bore him.

26 Also to punish the righteous is not good, nor to flog officials for their integrity.

27 He who spares his words has knowledge. He who is even tempered is a man of understanding.

28 Even a fool, when he keeps silent, is counted wise. When he shuts his lips, he is thought to be discerning.

Day 9 – Evening Sage Intake

We always need to be aware of the seductive attraction of gossip. It is constantly trying to lure us in, to listen and then rebroadcast what we hear. Perhaps it is because there is something in us that inappropriately feels better about ourselves when we hear how "bad" other people are. Yet, gossip can be so destructive. It destroys relationships, families, churches, and even communities. Instead of spreading gossip, let it stop with you. Whenever possible, don't listen. If you have heard gossip, don't repeat it. Instead, take a moment and privately pray for those involved.

Proverbs 18

1 An unfriendly man pursues selfishness, and defies all sound judgement.
2 A fool has no delight in understanding, but only in revealing his own opinion.
3 When wickedness comes, contempt also comes, and with shame comes disgrace.
4 The words of a man's mouth are like deep waters. The fountain of wisdom is like a flowing brook.
5 To be partial to the faces of the wicked is not good, nor to deprive the innocent of justice.
6 A fool's lips come into strife, and his mouth invites beatings.
7 A fool's mouth is his destruction, and his lips are a snare to his soul.
8 The words of a gossip are like dainty morsels: they go down into a person's innermost parts.
9 One who is slack in his work is brother to him who is a master of destruction.
10 The LORD's name is a strong tower: the righteous run to him, and are safe.
11 The rich man's wealth is his strong city, like an unscalable wall in his own imagination.
12 Before destruction the heart of man is proud, but before honor is humility.
13 He who gives answer before he hears, that is folly and shame to him.
14 A man's spirit will sustain him in sickness, but a crushed spirit, who can bear?
15 The heart of the discerning gets knowledge. The ear of the wise seeks knowledge.
16 A man's gift makes room for him, and brings him before great men.
17 He who pleads his cause first seems right; until another comes and questions him.
18 The lot settles disputes, and keeps strong ones apart.
19 A brother offended is more difficult than a fortified city; and disputes are like the bars of a fortress.
20 A man's stomach is filled with the fruit of his mouth. With the harvest of his lips he is satisfied.

21 Death and life are in the power of the tongue; those who love it will eat its fruit.

22 Whoever finds a wife finds a good thing, and obtains favor of the LORD.

23 The poor plead for mercy, but the rich answer harshly.

24 A man of many companions may be ruined, but there is a friend who sticks closer than a brother.

Day 10 – Morning Sage Intake

Ephesians 4:25 – Therefore putting away falsehood, speak truth each one with his neighbor. For we are members of one another.

Proverbs 19

1 Better is the poor who walks in his integrity than he who is perverse in his lips and is a fool.

2 It isn't good to have zeal without knowledge; nor being hasty with one's feet and missing the way.

3 The foolishness of man subverts his way; his heart rages against the LORD.

4 Wealth adds many friends, but the poor is separated from his friend.

5 A false witness shall not be unpunished. He who pours out lies shall not go free.

6 Many will entreat the favor of a ruler, and everyone is a friend to a man who gives gifts.

7 All the relatives of the poor shun him: how much more do his friends avoid him! He pursues them with pleas, but they are gone.

8 He who gets wisdom loves his own soul. He who keeps understanding shall find good.

9 A false witness shall not be unpunished. He who utters lies shall perish.

10 Delicate living is not appropriate for a fool, much less for a servant to have rule over princes.

11 The discretion of a man makes him slow to anger. It is his glory to overlook an offense.

12 The king's wrath is like the roaring of a lion, but his favor is like dew on the grass.

13 A foolish son is the calamity of his father. A wife's quarrels are a continual dripping.

14 House and riches are an inheritance from fathers, but a prudent wife is from the LORD.

15 Slothfulness casts into a deep sleep. The idle soul shall suffer hunger.

16 He who keeps the commandment keeps his soul, but he who is contemptuous in his ways shall die.

17 He who has pity on the poor lends to the LORD; he will reward him.

18 Discipline your son, for there is hope; don't be a willing party to his death.

19 A hot-tempered man must pay the penalty, for if you rescue him, you must do it again.

20 Listen to counsel and receive instruction, that you may be wise in your latter end.

21 There are many plans in a man's heart, but the LORD's counsel will prevail.

22 That which makes a man to be desired is his kindness. A poor man is better than a liar.

23 The fear of the LORD leads to life, then contentment; he rests and will not be touched by trouble.

24 The sluggard buries his hand in the dish; he will not so much as bring it to his mouth again.

25 Flog a scoffer, and the simple will learn prudence; rebuke one who has understanding, and he will gain knowledge.

26 He who robs his father and drives away his mother, is a son who causes shame and brings reproach.

27 If you stop listening to instruction, my son, you will stray from the words of knowledge.

28 A corrupt witness mocks justice, and the mouth of the wicked gulps down iniquity.

29 Penalties are prepared for scoffers, and beatings for the backs of fools.

Day 10 – Evening Sage Intake

I don't know about you, but verse 1 brings up a lot of bad memories for me. I am so thankful for a new life in Christ filled with the Holy Spirit! Ephesians 5:18-20 – Don't be drunk with wine, in which is dissipation, but be filled with the Spirit, speaking to one another in psalms, hymns, and spiritual songs; singing, and making melody in your heart to the Lord; always giving thanks to God the Father for everything, in the name of our Lord Jesus Christ.

Proverbs 20

1 Wine is a mocker, and beer is a brawler. Whoever is led astray by them is not wise.

2 The terror of a king is like the roaring of a lion. He who provokes him to anger forfeits his own life.

3 It is an honor for a man to keep aloof from strife; but every fool will be quarreling.

4 The sluggard will not plow by reason of the winter; therefore he shall beg in harvest, and have nothing.

5 Counsel in the heart of man is like deep water; but a man of understanding will draw it out.

6 Many men claim to be men of unfailing love, but who can find a faithful man?

7 A righteous man walks in integrity. Blessed are his children after him.

8 A king who sits on the throne of judgement scatters away all evil with his eyes.

9 Who can say, "I have made my heart pure. I am clean and without sin?"

10 Differing weights and differing measures, both of them alike are an abomination to the LORD.

11 Even a child makes himself known by his doings, whether his work is pure, and whether it is right.

12 The hearing ear, and the seeing eye, the LORD has made even both of them.

13 Don't love sleep, lest you come to poverty. Open your eyes, and you shall be satisfied with bread.

14 "It's no good, it's no good," says the buyer; but when he is gone his way, then he boasts.

15 There is gold and abundance of rubies; but the lips of knowledge are a rare jewel.

16 Take the garment of one who puts up collateral for a stranger; and hold him in pledge for a wayward woman.

17 Fraudulent food is sweet to a man, but afterwards his mouth is filled with gravel.

18 Plans are established by advice; by wise guidance you wage war!

19 He who goes about as a tale-bearer reveals secrets; therefore don't keep company with him who opens wide his lips.

20 Whoever curses his father or his mother, his lamp shall be put out in blackness of darkness.

21 An inheritance quickly gained at the beginning, won't be blessed in the end.

22 Don't say, "I will pay back evil." Wait for the LORD, and he will save you.

23 The LORD detests differing weights, and dishonest scales are not pleasing.

24 A man's steps are from the LORD; how then can man understand his way?

25 It is a snare to a man to make a rash dedication, then later to consider his vows.

26 A wise king winnows out the wicked, and drives the threshing wheel over them.

27 The spirit of man is the LORD's lamp, searching all his innermost parts.

28 Love and faithfulness keep the king safe. His throne is sustained by love.

29 The glory of young men is their strength. The splendor of old men is their grey hair.

30 Wounding blows cleanse away evil, and beatings purge the innermost parts.

Day 11 – Morning Sage Intake

God wants to perform spiritual heart surgery on all of us through the Holy Spirit. Ezekiel 36:26 – I will also give you a new heart, and I will put a new spirit within you; and I will take away the stony heart out of your flesh, and I will give you a heart of flesh. Soften our hearts Lord!

Proverbs 21

1 The king's heart is in the LORD's hand like the watercourses. He turns it wherever he desires.
2 Every way of a man is right in his own eyes, but the LORD weighs the hearts.
3 To do righteousness and justice is more acceptable to the LORD than sacrifice.
4 A high look, and a proud heart, the lamp of the wicked, is sin.
5 The plans of the diligent surely lead to profit; and everyone who is hasty surely rushes to poverty.
6 Getting treasures by a lying tongue is a fleeting vapor for those who seek death.
7 The violence of the wicked will drive them away, because they refuse to do what is right.
8 The way of the guilty is devious, but the conduct of the innocent is upright.
9 It is better to dwell in the corner of the housetop, than to share a house with a contentious woman.
10 The soul of the wicked desires evil; his neighbor finds no mercy in his eyes.
11 When the mocker is punished, the simple gains wisdom. When the wise is instructed, he receives knowledge.
12 The Righteous One considers the house of the wicked, and brings the wicked to ruin.
13 Whoever stops his ears at the cry of the poor, he will also cry out, but shall not be heard.
14 A gift in secret pacifies anger; and a bribe in the cloak, strong wrath.
15 It is joy to the righteous to do justice; but it is a destruction to the

workers of iniquity.

16 The man who wanders out of the way of understanding shall rest in the assembly of the departed spirits.

17 He who loves pleasure shall be a poor man. He who loves wine and oil shall not be rich.

18 The wicked is a ransom for the righteous; the treacherous for the upright.

19 It is better to dwell in a desert land, than with a contentious and fretful woman.

20 There is precious treasure and oil in the dwelling of the wise; but a foolish man swallows it up.

21 He who follows after righteousness and kindness finds life, righteousness, and honor.

22 A wise man scales the city of the mighty, and brings down the strength of its confidence.

23 Whoever guards his mouth and his tongue keeps his soul from troubles.

24 The proud and haughty man, "scoffer" is his name; he works in the arrogance of pride.

25 The desire of the sluggard kills him, for his hands refuse to labor.

26 There are those who covet greedily all day long; but the righteous give and don't withhold.

27 The sacrifice of the wicked is an abomination: how much more, when he brings it with a wicked mind!

28 A false witness will perish, and a man who listens speaks to eternity.

29 A wicked man hardens his face; but as for the upright, he establishes his ways.

30 There is no wisdom nor understanding nor counsel against the LORD.

31 The horse is prepared for the day of battle; but victory is with the LORD.

Day 11 – Evening Sage Intake

You might find it interesting to note that beginning with Proverbs 22:22 and continuing on through Proverbs 24:12, the proverbs are generally expressed in two verses instead of one.

Proverbs 22

1 A good name is more desirable than great riches, and enjoying favor is better than silver and gold.

2 The rich and the poor have this in common: The LORD is the maker of them all.

3 A prudent man sees danger, and hides himself; but the simple pass on, and suffer for it.

4 The result of humility and the fear of the LORD is wealth, honor, and life.

5 Thorns and snares are in the path of the wicked: whoever guards his soul stays from them.

6 Train up a child in the way he should go, and when he is old he will not depart from it.

7 The rich rule over the poor. The borrower is servant to the lender.

8 He who sows wickedness reaps trouble, and the rod of his fury will be destroyed.

9 He who has a generous eye will be blessed; for he shares his food with the poor.

10 Drive out the mocker, and strife will go out; yes, quarrels and insults will stop.

11 He who loves purity of heart and speaks gracefully is the king's friend.

12 The LORD's eyes watch over knowledge; but he frustrates the words of the unfaithful.

13 The sluggard says, "There is a lion outside! I will be killed in the streets!"

14 The mouth of an adulteress is a deep pit: he who is under the LORD's wrath will fall into it.

15 Folly is bound up in the heart of a child: the rod of discipline drives it far from him.

16 Whoever oppresses the poor for his own increase and whoever gives to the rich, both come to poverty.

17 Turn your ear, and listen to the words of the wise. Apply your heart to my teaching.

18 For it is a pleasant thing if you keep them within you, if all of them are ready on your lips.

19 That your trust may be in the LORD, I teach you today, even you.

20 Haven't I written to you thirty excellent things of counsel and

knowledge,

21 To teach you truth, reliable words, to give sound answers to the ones who sent you?

22 Don't exploit the poor, because he is poor; and don't crush the needy in court;

23 for the LORD will plead their case, and plunder the life of those who plunder them.

24 Don't befriend a hot-tempered man, and don't associate with one who harbors anger:

25 lest you learn his ways, and ensnare your soul.

26 Don't you be one of those who strike hands, of those who are collateral for debts.

27 If you don't have means to pay, why should he take away your bed from under you?

28 Don't move the ancient boundary stone, which your fathers have set up.

29 Do you see a man skilled in his work? He will serve kings. He won't serve obscure men.

Day 12 – Morning Sage Intake

Fix your eyes on Jesus and give Him your heart!

Proverbs 23

1 When you sit to eat with a ruler, consider diligently what is before you;

2 put a knife to your throat, if you are a man given to appetite.

3 Don't be desirous of his dainties, since they are deceitful food.

4 Don't weary yourself to be rich. In your wisdom, show restraint.

5 Why do you set your eyes on that which is not? For it certainly sprouts wings like an eagle and flies in the sky.

6 Don't eat the food of him who has a stingy eye, and don't crave his delicacies:

7 for as he thinks about the cost, so he is. "Eat and drink!" he says to you, but his heart is not with you.

8 The morsel which you have eaten you shall vomit up, and lose your good words.

9 Don't speak in the ears of a fool, for he will despise the wisdom of your words.

10 Don't move the ancient boundary stone. Don't encroach on the fields of the fatherless:

11 for their Defender is strong. He will plead their case against you.

12 Apply your heart to instruction, and your ears to the words of knowledge.

13 Don't withhold correction from a child. If you punish him with the rod, he will not die.

14 Punish him with the rod, and save his soul from Sheol.

15 My son, if your heart is wise, then my heart will be glad, even mine:

16 yes, my heart will rejoice, when your lips speak what is right.

17 Don't let your heart envy sinners; but rather fear the LORD all the day long.

18 Indeed surely there is a future hope, and your hope will not be cut off.

19 Listen, my son, and be wise, and keep your heart on the right path!

20 Don't be amongst ones drinking too much wine, or those who gorge themselves on meat:

21 for the drunkard and the glutton shall become poor; and drowsiness clothes them in rags.

22 Listen to your father who gave you life, and don't despise your mother when she is old.

23 Buy the truth, and don't sell it. Get wisdom, discipline, and understanding.

24 The father of the righteous has great joy. Whoever fathers a wise child delights in him.

25 Let your father and your mother be glad! Let her who bore you rejoice!

26 My son, give me your heart; and let your eyes keep in my ways.

27 For a prostitute is a deep pit; and a wayward wife is a narrow well.

28 Yes, she lies in wait like a robber, and increases the unfaithful amongst men.

29 Who has woe? Who has sorrow? Who has strife? Who has complaints? Who has needless bruises? Who has bloodshot eyes?

30 Those who stay long at the wine; those who go to seek out mixed wine.

31 Don't look at the wine when it is red, when it sparkles in the cup,

when it goes down smoothly.

32 In the end, it bites like a snake, and poisons like a viper.

33 Your eyes will see strange things, and your mind will imagine confusing things.

34 Yes, you will be as he who lies down in the middle of the sea, or as he who lies on top of the rigging:

35 "They hit me, and I was not hurt! They beat me, and I don't feel it! When will I wake up? I can do it again. I can find another."

Day 12 – Evening Sage Intake

As sweet as honey is to our lips, the Word and wisdom of God is to our soul!

Proverbs 24

1 Don't be envious of evil men; neither desire to be with them:

2 for their hearts plot violence, and their lips talk about mischief.

3 Through wisdom a house is built; by understanding it is established;

4 by knowledge the rooms are filled with all rare and beautiful treasure.

5 A wise man has great power; and a knowledgeable man increases strength;

6 for by wise guidance you wage your war; and victory is in many advisers.

7 Wisdom is too high for a fool: he doesn't open his mouth in the gate.

8 One who plots to do evil will be called a schemer.

9 The schemes of folly are sin. The mocker is detested by men.

10 If you falter in the time of trouble, your strength is small.

11 Rescue those who are being led away to death! Indeed, hold back those who are staggering to the slaughter!

12 If you say, "Behold, we didn't know this"; doesn't he who weighs the hearts consider it? He who keeps your soul, doesn't he know it? Shall he not render to every man according to his work?

13 My son, eat honey, for it is good; the droppings of the honeycomb, which are sweet to your taste:

14 so you shall know wisdom to be to your soul; if you have found it,

then there will be a reward, your hope will not be cut off.

15 Don't lay in wait, wicked man, against the habitation of the righteous. Don't destroy his resting place:

16 for a righteous man falls seven times, and rises up again; but the wicked are overthrown by calamity.

17 Don't rejoice when your enemy falls. Don't let your heart be glad when he is overthrown;

18 lest the LORD see it, and it displease him, and he turn away his wrath from him.

19 Don't fret yourself because of evildoers; neither be envious of the wicked:

20 for there will be no reward to the evil man; and the lamp of the wicked shall be snuffed out.

21 My son, fear the LORD and the king. Don't join those who are rebellious:

22 for their calamity will rise suddenly; the destruction from them both—who knows?

23 These also are sayings of the wise. To show partiality in judgement is not good.

24 He who says to the wicked, "You are righteous"; peoples shall curse him, and nations shall abhor him—

25 but it will go well with those who convict the guilty, and a rich blessing will come on them.

26 An honest answer is like a kiss on the lips.

27 Prepare your work outside, and get your fields ready. Afterwards, build your house.

28 Don't be a witness against your neighbor without cause. Don't deceive with your lips.

29 Don't say, "I will do to him as he has done to me; I will render to the man according to his work."

30 I went by the field of the sluggard, by the vineyard of the man void of understanding;

31 Behold, it was all grown over with thorns. Its surface was covered with nettles, and its stone wall was broken down.

32 Then I saw, and considered well. I saw, and received instruction:

33 a little sleep, a little slumber, a little folding of the hands to sleep;

34 so your poverty will come as a robber, and your want as an armed man.

Day 13 – Morning Sage Intake

Verse 1 of Proverbs 25 is the title of a collection of Solomon's proverbs (25:1-29:27) which were apparently transferred from another source during the days of Hezekiah.

Proverbs 25

1 These also are proverbs of Solomon, which the men of Hezekiah king of Judah copied out.

2 It is the glory of God to conceal a thing, but the glory of kings is to search out a matter.

3 As the heavens for height, and the earth for depth, so the hearts of kings are unsearchable.

4 Take away the dross from the silver, and material comes out for the refiner;

5 Take away the wicked from the king's presence, and his throne will be established in righteousness.

6 Don't exalt yourself in the presence of the king, or claim a place amongst great men;

7 for it is better that it be said to you, "Come up here," than that you should be put lower in the presence of the prince, whom your eyes have seen.

8 Don't be hasty in bringing charges to court. What will you do in the end when your neighbor shames you?

9 Debate your case with your neighbor, and don't betray the confidence of another;

10 lest one who hears it put you to shame, and your bad reputation never depart.

11 A word fitly spoken is like apples of gold in settings of silver.

12 As an earring of gold, and an ornament of fine gold, so is a wise man's rebuke to an obedient ear.

13 As the cold of snow in the time of harvest, so is a faithful messenger to those who send him; for he refreshes the soul of his masters.

14 As clouds and wind without rain, so is he who boasts of gifts deceptively.

15 By patience a ruler is persuaded. A soft tongue breaks the bone.

16 Have you found honey? Eat as much as is sufficient for you, lest you eat too much, and vomit it.

17 Let your foot be seldom in your neighbor's house, lest he be weary of you, and hate you.

18 A man who gives false testimony against his neighbor is like a club, a sword, or a sharp arrow.

19 Confidence in someone unfaithful in time of trouble is like a bad tooth, or a lame foot.

20 As one who takes away a garment in cold weather, or vinegar on soda, so is one who sings songs to a heavy heart.

21 If your enemy is hungry, give him food to eat. If he is thirsty, give him water to drink:

22 for you will heap coals of fire on his head, and the LORD will reward you.

23 The north wind produces rain: so a backbiting tongue brings an angry face.

24 It is better to dwell in the corner of the housetop, than to share a house with a contentious woman.

25 Like cold water to a thirsty soul, so is good news from a far country.

26 Like a muddied spring, and a polluted well, so is a righteous man who gives way before the wicked.

27 It is not good to eat much honey; nor is it honorable to seek one's own honor.

28 Like a city that is broken down and without walls is a man whose spirit is without restraint.

Day 13 – Evening Sage Intake

Never argue with a fool. They drag you down to their level and then beat you with experience!

Proverbs 26

1 Like snow in summer, and as rain in harvest, so honor is not fitting for a fool.

2 Like a fluttering sparrow, like a darting swallow, so the undeserved curse doesn't come to rest.

3 A whip is for the horse, a bridle for the donkey, and a rod for the back of fools!

4 Don't answer a fool according to his folly, lest you also be like him.

5 Answer a fool according to his folly, lest he be wise in his own eyes.

6 One who sends a message by the hand of a fool is cutting off his own feet and drinking violence.

7 Like the legs of the lame that hang loose: so is a parable in the mouth of fools.

8 As one who binds a stone in a sling, so is he who gives honor to a fool.

9 Like a thorn bush that goes into the hand of a drunkard, so is a parable in the mouth of fools.

10 As an archer who wounds all, so is he who hires a fool or he who hires those who pass by.

11 As a dog that returns to his vomit, so is a fool who repeats his folly.

12 Do you see a man wise in his own eyes? There is more hope for a fool than for him.

13 The sluggard says, "There is a lion in the road! A fierce lion roams the streets!"

14 As the door turns on its hinges, so does the sluggard on his bed.

15 The sluggard buries his hand in the dish. He is too lazy to bring it back to his mouth.

16 The sluggard is wiser in his own eyes than seven men who answer with discretion.

17 Like one who grabs a dog's ears is one who passes by and meddles in a quarrel not his own.

18 Like a madman who shoots torches, arrows, and death,

19 is the man who deceives his neighbor and says, "Am I not joking?"

20 For lack of wood a fire goes out. Without gossip, a quarrel dies down.

21 As coals are to hot embers, and wood to fire, so is a contentious man to kindling strife.

22 The words of a whisperer are as dainty morsels, they go down into the innermost parts.

23 Like silver dross on an earthen vessel are the lips of a fervent one with an evil heart.

24 A malicious man disguises himself with his lips, but he harbors

evil in his heart.

25 When his speech is charming, don't believe him; for there are seven abominations in his heart.

26 His malice may be concealed by deception, but his wickedness will be exposed in the assembly.

27 Whoever digs a pit shall fall into it. Whoever rolls a stone, it will come back on him.

28 A lying tongue hates those it hurts; and a flattering mouth works ruin.

Day 14 – Morning Sage Intake

Matthew 6:33-34a – But seek first God's Kingdom, and his righteousness; and all these things will be given to you as well. Therefore don't be anxious for tomorrow, for tomorrow will be anxious for itself. (Deo volente)

Proverbs 27

1 Don't boast about tomorrow; for you don't know what a day may bring.

2 Let another man praise you, and not your own mouth; a stranger, and not your own lips.

3 A stone is heavy, and sand is a burden; but a fool's provocation is heavier than both.

4 Wrath is cruel, and anger is overwhelming; but who is able to stand before jealousy?

5 Better is open rebuke than hidden love.

6 Faithful are the wounds of a friend; although the kisses of an enemy are profuse.

7 A full soul loathes a honeycomb; but to a hungry soul, every bitter thing is sweet.

8 As a bird that wanders from her nest, so is a man who wanders from his home.

9 Perfume and incense bring joy to the heart; so does earnest counsel from a man's friend.

10 Don't forsake your friend and your father's friend. Don't go to your brother's house in the day of your disaster: better is a neighbor

who is near than a distant brother.

11 Be wise, my son, and bring joy to my heart, then I can answer my tormentor.

12 A prudent man sees danger and takes refuge; but the simple pass on, and suffer for it.

13 Take his garment when he puts up collateral for a stranger. Hold it for a wayward woman!

14 He who blesses his neighbor with a loud voice early in the morning, it will be taken as a curse by him.

15 A continual dropping on a rainy day and a contentious wife are alike:

16 restraining her is like restraining the wind, or like grasping oil in his right hand.

17 Iron sharpens iron; so a man sharpens his friend's countenance.

18 Whoever tends the fig tree shall eat its fruit. He who looks after his master shall be honored.

19 Like water reflects a face, so a man's heart reflects the man.

20 Sheol and Abaddon are never satisfied; and a man's eyes are never satisfied.

21 The crucible is for silver, and the furnace for gold; but man is refined by his praise.

22 Though you grind a fool in a mortar with a pestle along with grain, yet his foolishness will not be removed from him.

23 Know well the state of your flocks, and pay attention to your herds:

24 for riches are not forever, nor does even the crown endure to all generations.

25 The hay is removed, and the new growth appears, the grasses of the hills are gathered in.

26 The lambs are for your clothing, and the goats are the price of a field.

27 There will be plenty of goats' milk for your food, for your family's food, and for the nourishment of your servant girls.

Day 14 – Evening Sage Intake

Verse 13 reminds me of one of my all time favorite Bible verses:
1 John 1:9 – If we confess our sins, he is faithful and righteous to
forgive us the sins, and to cleanse us from all unrighteousness.

Proverbs 28

1 The wicked flee when no one pursues; but the righteous are as bold
as a lion.
2 In rebellion, a land has many rulers, but order is maintained by a
man of understanding and knowledge.
3 A needy man who oppresses the poor is like a driving rain which
leaves no crops.
4 Those who forsake the law praise the wicked; but those who keep
the law contend with them.
5 Evil men don't understand justice; but those who seek the LORD
understand it fully.
6 Better is the poor who walks in his integrity, than he who is
perverse in his ways, and he is rich.
7 Whoever keeps the law is a wise son; but he who is a companion of
gluttons shames his father.
8 He who increases his wealth by excessive interest gathers it for one
who has pity on the poor.
9 He who turns away his ear from hearing the law, even his prayer is
an abomination.
10 Whoever causes the upright to go astray in an evil way, he will fall
into his own trap; but the blameless will inherit good.
11 The rich man is wise in his own eyes; but the poor who has
understanding sees through him.
12 When the righteous triumph, there is great glory; but when the
wicked rise, men hide themselves.
13 He who conceals his sins doesn't prosper, but whoever confesses
and renounces them finds mercy.
14 Blessed is the man who always fears; but one who hardens his
heart falls into trouble.
15 As a roaring lion or a charging bear, so is a wicked ruler over
helpless people.

16 A tyrannical ruler lacks judgement. One who hates ill-gotten gain will have long days.

17 A man who is tormented by life blood will be a fugitive until death; no one will support him.

18 Whoever walks blamelessly is kept safe; but one with perverse ways will fall suddenly.

19 One who works his land will have an abundance of food; but one who chases fantasies will have his fill of poverty.

20 A faithful man is rich with blessings; but one who is eager to be rich will not go unpunished.

21 To show partiality is not good; yet a man will do wrong for a piece of bread.

22 A stingy man hurries after riches, and doesn't know that poverty waits for him.

23 One who rebukes a man will afterward find more favor than one who flatters with the tongue.

24 Whoever robs his father or his mother, and says, "It's not wrong." He is a partner with a destroyer.

25 One who is greedy stirs up strife; but one who trusts in the LORD will prosper.

26 One who trusts in himself is a fool; but one who walks in wisdom is kept safe.

27 One who gives to the poor has no lack; but one who closes his eyes will have many curses.

28 When the wicked rise, men hide themselves; but when they perish, the righteous thrive.

This is the end of the second week! You are doing great. Remember, you are the light of the world!

Day 15 – Morning Sage Intake

I am constantly reminding people of the importance of spending time reading the Bible. I would encourage you again today to make it a priority in your daily life. But knowing the Bible is not the only goal, applying what God teaches us in His word in our daily lives is what enables us to experience real now and forever life in His story and be the "light of the world".

Proverbs 29

1 He who is often rebuked and stiffens his neck will be destroyed suddenly, with no remedy.
2 When the righteous thrive, the people rejoice; but when the wicked rule, the people groan.
3 Whoever loves wisdom brings joy to his father; but a companion of prostitutes squanders his wealth.
4 The king by justice makes the land stable, but he who takes bribes tears it down.
5 A man who flatters his neighbor spreads a net for his feet.
6 An evil man is snared by his sin, but the righteous can sing and be glad.
7 The righteous care about justice for the poor. The wicked aren't concerned about knowledge.
8 Mockers stir up a city, but wise men turn away anger.
9 If a wise man goes to court with a foolish man, the fool rages or scoffs, and there is no peace.
10 The bloodthirsty hate a man of integrity; and they seek the life of the upright.
11 A fool vents all of his anger, but a wise man brings himself under control.
12 If a ruler listens to lies, all of his officials are wicked.
13 The poor man and the oppressor have this in common: The LORD gives sight to the eyes of both.
14 The king who fairly judges the poor, his throne shall be established forever.
15 The rod of correction gives wisdom, but a child left to himself causes shame to his mother.

16 When the wicked increase, sin increases; but the righteous will see their downfall.

17 Correct your son, and he will give you peace; yes, he will bring delight to your soul.

18 Where there is no revelation, the people cast off restraint; but one who keeps the law is blessed.

19 A servant can't be corrected by words. Though he understands, yet he will not respond.

20 Do you see a man who is hasty in his words? There is more hope for a fool than for him.

21 He who pampers his servant from youth will have him become a son in the end.

22 An angry man stirs up strife, and a wrathful man abounds in sin.

23 A man's pride brings him low, but one of lowly spirit gains honor.

24 Whoever is an accomplice of a thief is an enemy of his own soul. He takes an oath, but dares not testify.

25 The fear of man proves to be a snare, but whoever puts his trust in the LORD is kept safe.

26 Many seek the ruler's favor, but a man's justice comes from the LORD.

27 A dishonest man detests the righteous, and the upright in their ways detest the wicked.

Day 15 – Evening Sage Intake

While the first 29 chapters of Proverbs are attributed to Solomon, Chapter 30 and Chapter 31 have different authors. Both chapters are still considered to be divinely inspired. Proverbs 30 is attributed to Agur, the son of Jakeh.

Proverbs 30

1 The words of Agur the son of Jakeh, the revelation: the man says to Ithiel, to Ithiel and Ucal:

2 "Surely I am the most ignorant man, and don't have a man's understanding.

3 I have not learned wisdom, neither do I have the knowledge of the Holy One.

4 Who has ascended up into heaven, and descended? Who has gathered the wind in his fists? Who has bound the waters in his garment? Who has established all the ends of the earth? What is his name, and what is his son's name, if you know?

5 "Every word of God is flawless. He is a shield to those who take refuge in him.

6 Don't you add to his words, lest he reprove you, and you be found a liar.

7 "Two things I have asked of you; don't deny me before I die:

8 remove far from me falsehood and lies. Give me neither poverty nor riches. Feed me with the food that is needful for me;

9 lest I be full, deny you, and say, 'Who is the LORD?' or lest I be poor, and steal, and so dishonor the name of my God.

10 "Don't slander a servant to his master, lest he curse you, and you be held guilty.

11 There is a generation that curses their father, and doesn't bless their mother.

12 There is a generation that is pure in their own eyes, yet are not washed from their filthiness.

13 There is a generation, oh how lofty are their eyes! Their eyelids are lifted up.

14 There is a generation whose teeth are like swords, and their jaws like knives, to devour the poor from the earth, and the needy from amongst men.

15 "The leach has two daughters: 'Give, give.' "There are three things that are never satisfied; four that don't say, 'Enough:'

16 Sheol, the barren womb; the earth that is not satisfied with water; and the fire that doesn't say, 'Enough.'

17 "The eye that mocks at his father, and scorns obedience to his mother: the ravens of the valley shall pick it out, the young eagles shall eat it.

18 "There are three things which are too amazing for me, four which I don't understand:

19 the way of an eagle in the air; the way of a serpent on a rock; the way of a ship in the middle of the sea; and the way of a man with a maiden.

20 "So is the way of an adulterous woman: she eats and wipes her mouth, and says, 'I have done nothing wrong.'

21 "For three things the earth tremble, and under four, it can't bear

up:

22 for a servant when he is king; a fool when he is filled with food;

23 for an unloved woman when she is married; and a servant who is heir to her mistress.

24 "There are four things which are little on the earth, but they are exceedingly wise:

25 the ants are not a strong people, yet they provide their food in the summer.

26 The conies are but a feeble folk, yet they make their houses in the rocks.

27 The locusts have no king, yet they advance in ranks.

28 You can catch a lizard with your hands, yet it is in kings' palaces.

29 "There are three things which are stately in their march, four which are stately in going:

30 the lion, which is mightiest amongst animals, and doesn't turn away for any;

31 the greyhound, the male goat also; and the king against whom there is no rising up.

32 "If you have done foolishly in lifting up yourself, or if you have thought evil, put your hand over your mouth.

33 For as the churning of milk produces butter, and the wringing of the nose produces blood; so the forcing of wrath produces strife."

Day 16 – Morning Sage Intake

The first verse of Proverbs 31 lists King Lemuel as its author. Some believe that King Lemuel is actually King Solomon. Lemuel, which means "devoted to God", was apparently used as an affectionate name. It is speculated that this was an affectionate name that was given to Solomon by his mother. While we are not sure of the true identity of King Lemuel, we are confident that Proverbs 31 is divinely inspired!

Proverbs 31

1 The words of king Lemuel; the revelation which his mother taught him.

2 "Oh, my son! Oh, son of my womb! Oh, son of my vows!

3 Don't give your strength to women, nor your ways to that which destroys kings.

4 It is not for kings, Lemuel; it is not for kings to drink wine; nor for princes to say, 'Where is strong drink?'

5 Lest they drink, and forget the law, and pervert the justice due to anyone who is afflicted.

6 Give strong drink to him who is ready to perish; and wine to the bitter in soul:

7 Let him drink, and forget his poverty, and remember his misery no more.

8 Open your mouth for the mute, in the cause of all who are left desolate.

9 Open your mouth, judge righteously, and serve justice to the poor and needy."

10 Who can find a worthy woman? For her price is far above rubies.

11 The heart of her husband trusts in her. He shall have no lack of gain.

12 She does him good, and not harm, all the days of her life.

13 She seeks wool and flax, and works eagerly with her hands.

14 She is like the merchant ships. She brings her bread from afar.

15 She rises also while it is yet night, gives food to her household, and portions for her servant girls.

16 She considers a field, and buys it. With the fruit of her hands, she plants a vineyard.

17 She arms her waist with strength, and makes her arms strong.

18 She perceives that her merchandise is profitable. Her lamp doesn't go out by night.

19 She lays her hands to the distaff, and her hands hold the spindle.

20 She opens her arms to the poor; yes, she extends her hands to the needy.

21 She is not afraid of the snow for her household; for all her household are clothed with scarlet.

22 She makes for herself carpets of tapestry. Her clothing is fine linen and purple.

23 Her husband is respected in the gates, when he sits amongst the elders of the land.

24 She makes linen garments and sells them, and delivers sashes to the merchant.

25 Strength and dignity are her clothing. She laughs at the time to

come.

26 She opens her mouth with wisdom. Faithful instruction is on her tongue.

27 She looks well to the ways of her household, and doesn't eat the bread of idleness.

28 Her children rise up and call her blessed. Her husband also praises her:

29 "Many women do noble things, but you excel them all."

30 Charm is deceitful, and beauty is vain; but a woman who fears the LORD, she shall be praised.

31 Give her of the fruit of her hands! Let her works praise her in the gates!

Day 16 – Evening Sage Intake

Verse 33 reminds us that real now and forever life is found in listening to His word and walking in His way!

Proverbs 1

1 The proverbs of Solomon, the son of David, king of Israel:

2 to know wisdom and instruction; to discern the words of understanding;

3 to receive instruction in wise dealing, in righteousness, justice, and equity;

4 to give prudence to the simple, knowledge and discretion to the young man:

5 that the wise man may hear, and increase in learning; that the man of understanding may attain to sound counsel:

6 to understand a proverb, and parables, the words and riddles of the wise.

7 The fear of the LORD is the beginning of knowledge; but the foolish despise wisdom and instruction.

8 My son, listen to your father's instruction, and don't forsake your mother's teaching:

9 for they will be a garland to grace your head, and chains around your neck.

10 My son, if sinners entice you, don't consent.

11 If they say, "Come with us, Let's lay in wait for blood; let's lurk secretly for the innocent without cause;

12 let's swallow them up alive like Sheol, and whole, like those who go down into the pit.

13 We'll find all valuable wealth. We'll fill our houses with plunder.

14 You shall cast your lot amongst us. We'll all have one purse."

15 My son, don't walk on the path with them. Keep your foot from their path,

16 for their feet run to evil. They hurry to shed blood.

17 For in vain is the net spread in the sight of any bird:

18 but these lay wait for their own blood. They lurk secretly for their own lives.

19 So are the ways of everyone who is greedy for gain. It takes away the life of its owners.

20 Wisdom calls aloud in the street. She utters her voice in the public squares.

21 She calls at the head of noisy places. At the entrance of the city gates, she utters her words:

22 "How long, you simple ones, will you love simplicity? How long will mockers delight themselves in mockery, and fools hate knowledge?

23 Turn at my reproof. Behold, I will pour out my spirit on you. I will make known my words to you.

24 Because I have called, and you have refused; I have stretched out my hand, and no one has paid attention;

25 but you have ignored all my counsel, and wanted none of my reproof;

26 I also will laugh at your disaster. I will mock when calamity overtakes you;

27 when calamity overtakes you like a storm, when your disaster comes on like a whirlwind; when distress and anguish come on you.

28 Then will they call on me, but I will not answer. They will seek me diligently, but they will not find me;

29 because they hated knowledge, and didn't choose the fear of the LORD.

30 They wanted none of my counsel. They despised all my reproof.

31 Therefore they will eat of the fruit of their own way, and be filled with their own schemes.

32 For the backsliding of the simple will kill them. The careless ease

of fools will destroy them.

33 But whoever listens to me will dwell securely, and will be at ease, without fear of harm."

Day 17 – Morning Sage Intake

James 1:5 – But if any of you lacks wisdom, let him ask of God, who gives to all liberally and without reproach; and it will be given to him.

Proverbs 2

1 My son, if you will receive my words, and store up my commandments within you;

2 So as to turn your ear to wisdom, and apply your heart to understanding;

3 Yes, if you call out for discernment, and lift up your voice for understanding;

4 If you seek her as silver, and search for her as for hidden treasures:

5 then you will understand the fear of the LORD, and find the knowledge of God.

6 For the LORD gives wisdom. Out of his mouth comes knowledge and understanding.

7 He lays up sound wisdom for the upright. He is a shield to those who walk in integrity;

8 that he may guard the paths of justice, and preserve the way of his saints.

9 Then you will understand righteousness and justice, equity and every good path.

10 For wisdom will enter into your heart. Knowledge will be pleasant to your soul.

11 Discretion will watch over you. Understanding will keep you,

12 to deliver you from the way of evil, from the men who speak perverse things;

13 who forsake the paths of uprightness, to walk in the ways of darkness;

14 who rejoice to do evil, and delight in the perverseness of evil;

15 who are crooked in their ways, and wayward in their paths:

16 To deliver you from the strange woman, even from the foreigner who flatters with her words;

17 who forsakes the friend of her youth, and forgets the covenant of her God:

18 for her house leads down to death, her paths to the departed spirits.

19 None who go to her return again, neither do they attain to the paths of life:

20 that you may walk in the way of good men, and keep the paths of the righteous.

21 For the upright will dwell in the land. The perfect will remain in it.

22 But the wicked will be cut off from the land. The treacherous will be rooted out of it.

Day 17 – Evening Sage Intake

James 3:13 – Who is wise and understanding amongst you? Let him show by his good conduct that his deeds are done in gentleness of wisdom.

Proverbs 3

1 My son, don't forget my teaching; but let your heart keep my commandments:

2 for length of days, and years of life, and peace, will they add to you.

3 Don't let kindness and truth forsake you. Bind them around your neck. Write them on the tablet of your heart.

4 So you will find favor and good understanding in the sight of God and man.

5 Trust in the LORD with all your heart, and don't lean on your own understanding.

6 In all your ways acknowledge him, and he will make your paths straight.

7 Don't be wise in your own eyes. Fear the LORD, and depart from evil.

8 It will be health to your body, and nourishment to your bones.

9 Honor the LORD with your substance, with the first fruits of all your increase:

10 so your barns will be filled with plenty, and your vats will

overflow with new wine.

11 My son, don't despise the LORD's discipline, neither be weary of his reproof:

12 for whom the LORD loves, he reproves; even as a father reproves the son in whom he delights.

13 Happy is the man who finds wisdom, the man who gets understanding.

14 For her good profit is better than getting silver, and her return is better than fine gold.

15 She is more precious than rubies. None of the things you can desire are to be compared to her.

16 Length of days is in her right hand. In her left hand are riches and honor.

17 Her ways are ways of pleasantness. All her paths are peace.

18 She is a tree of life to those who lay hold of her. Happy is everyone who retains her.

19 By wisdom the LORD founded the earth. By understanding, he established the heavens.

20 By his knowledge, the depths were broken up, and the skies drop down the dew.

21 My son, let them not depart from your eyes. Keep sound wisdom and discretion:

22 so they will be life to your soul, and grace for your neck.

23 Then you shall walk in your way securely. Your foot won't stumble.

24 When you lie down, you will not be afraid. Yes, you will lie down, and your sleep will be sweet.

25 Don't be afraid of sudden fear, neither of the desolation of the wicked, when it comes:

26 for the LORD will be your confidence, and will keep your foot from being taken.

27 Don't withhold good from those to whom it is due, when it is in the power of your hand to do it.

28 Don't say to your neighbor, "Go, and come again; tomorrow I will give it to you," when you have it by you.

29 Don't devise evil against your neighbor, since he dwells securely by you.

30 Don't strive with a man without cause, if he has done you no harm.

31 Don't envy the man of violence. Choose none of his ways.

32 For the perverse is an abomination to the LORD, but his friendship is with the upright.

33 The LORD's curse is in the house of the wicked, but he blesses the habitation of the righteous.

34 Surely he mocks the mockers, but he gives grace to the humble.

35 The wise will inherit glory, but shame will be the promotion of fools.

Day 18 – Morning Sage Intake

Deuteronomy 4:9 – Only be careful, and keep your soul diligently, lest you forget the things which your eyes saw, and lest they depart from your heart all the days of your life; but make them known to your children and your children's children;

Proverbs 4

1 Listen, sons, to a father's instruction. Pay attention and know understanding;

2 for I give you sound learning. Don't forsake my law.

3 For I was a son to my father, tender and an only child in the sight of my mother.

4 He taught me, and said to me: "Let your heart retain my words. Keep my commandments, and live.

5 Get wisdom. Get understanding. Don't forget, neither swerve from the words of my mouth.

6 Don't forsake her, and she will preserve you. Love her, and she will keep you.

7 Wisdom is supreme. Get wisdom. Yes, though it costs all your possessions, get understanding.

8 Esteem her, and she will exalt you. She will bring you to honor, when you embrace her.

9 She will give to your head a garland of grace. She will deliver a crown of splendor to you."

10 Listen, my son, and receive my sayings. The years of your life will be many.

11 I have taught you in the way of wisdom. I have led you in straight paths.

12 When you go, your steps will not be hampered. When you run, you will not stumble.

13 Take firm hold of instruction. Don't let her go. Keep her, for she is your life.

14 Don't enter into the path of the wicked. Don't walk in the way of evil men.

15 Avoid it, and don't pass by it. Turn from it, and pass on.

16 For they don't sleep, unless they do evil. Their sleep is taken away, unless they make someone fall.

17 For they eat the bread of wickedness, and drink the wine of violence.

18 But the path of the righteous is like the dawning light that shines more and more until the perfect day.

19 The way of the wicked is like darkness. They don't know what they stumble over.

20 My son, attend to my words. Turn your ear to my sayings.

21 Let them not depart from your eyes. Keep them in the center of your heart.

22 For they are life to those who find them, and health to their whole body.

23 Keep your heart with all diligence, for out of it is the wellspring of life.

24 Put away from yourself a perverse mouth. Put corrupt lips far from you.

25 Let your eyes look straight ahead. Fix your gaze directly before you.

26 Make the path of your feet level. Let all of your ways be established.

27 Don't turn to the right hand nor to the left. Remove your foot from evil.

Day 18 – Evening Sage Intake

If you have to make a decision based on what the Bible says about a subject, or based on what the culture has to say about a subject, I would go with the Bible. The culture is constantly changing. The Bible remains steady and true. Isaiah 40:8 says – The grass withers, the flower fades; but the word of our God stands forever."

Proverbs 5

1 My son, pay attention to my wisdom. Turn your ear to my understanding:

2 that you may maintain discretion, that your lips may preserve knowledge.

3 For the lips of an adulteress drip honey. Her mouth is smoother than oil,

4 but in the end she is as bitter as wormwood, and as sharp as a two-edged sword.

5 Her feet go down to death. Her steps lead straight to Sheol.

6 She gives no thought to the way of life. Her ways are crooked, and she doesn't know it.

7 Now therefore, my sons, listen to me. Don't depart from the words of my mouth.

8 Remove your way far from her. Don't come near the door of her house,

9 lest you give your honor to others, and your years to the cruel one;

10 lest strangers feast on your wealth, and your labors enrich another man's house.

11 You will groan at your latter end, when your flesh and your body are consumed,

12 and say, "How I have hated instruction, and my heart despised reproof;

13 neither have I obeyed the voice of my teachers, nor turned my ear to those who instructed me!

14 I have come to the brink of utter ruin, amongst the gathered assembly."

15 Drink water out of your own cistern, running water out of your own well.

16 Should your springs overflow in the streets, streams of water in the public squares?

17 Let them be for yourself alone, not for strangers with you.

18 Let your spring be blessed. Rejoice in the wife of your youth.

19 A loving doe and a graceful deer—let her breasts satisfy you at all times. Be captivated always with her love.

20 For why should you, my son, be captivated with an adulteress? Why embrace the bosom of another?

21 For the ways of man are before the LORD's eyes. He examines all

his paths.

22 The evil deeds of the wicked ensnare him. The cords of his sin hold him firmly.

23 He will die for lack of instruction. In the greatness of his folly, he will go astray.

Day 19 – Morning Sage Intake

We experience now and forever life as we realize that we were created for a purpose. Our lives have meaning. We have been called and tasked with a mission. We are ambassadors for Christ. Embrace your calling each day by being thankful for five things and encouraging two people. It is amazing to see what God can do with simple activities which are offered to Him with a little bit of faith.

Proverbs 6

1 My son, if you have become collateral for your neighbor, if you have struck your hands in pledge for a stranger;

2 You are trapped by the words of your mouth. You are ensnared with the words of your mouth.

3 Do this now, my son, and deliver yourself, since you have come into the hand of your neighbor. Go, humble yourself. Press your plea with your neighbor.

4 Give no sleep to your eyes, nor slumber to your eyelids.

5 Free yourself, like a gazelle from the hand of the hunter, like a bird from the snare of the fowler.

6 Go to the ant, you sluggard. Consider her ways, and be wise;

7 which having no chief, overseer, or ruler,

8 provides her bread in the summer, and gathers her food in the harvest.

9 How long will you sleep, sluggard? When will you arise out of your sleep?

10 A little sleep, a little slumber, a little folding of the hands to sleep:

11 so your poverty will come as a robber, and your scarcity as an armed man.

12 A worthless person, a man of iniquity, is he who walks with a perverse mouth;

13 who winks with his eyes, who signals with his feet, who motions with his fingers;

14 in whose heart is perverseness, who devises evil continually, who always sows discord.

15 Therefore his calamity will come suddenly. He will be broken suddenly, and that without remedy.

16 There are six things which the LORD hates; yes, seven which are an abomination to him:

17 haughty eyes, a lying tongue, hands that shed innocent blood;

18 a heart that devises wicked schemes, feet that are swift in running to mischief,

19 a false witness who utters lies, and he who sows discord amongst brothers.

20 My son, keep your father's commandment, and don't forsake your mother's teaching.

21 Bind them continually on your heart. Tie them around your neck.

22 When you walk, it will lead you. When you sleep, it will watch over you. When you awake, it will talk with you.

23 For the commandment is a lamp, and the law is light. Reproofs of instruction are the way of life,

24 to keep you from the immoral woman, from the flattery of the wayward wife's tongue.

25 Don't lust after her beauty in your heart, neither let her captivate you with her eyelids.

26 For a prostitute reduces you to a piece of bread. The adulteress hunts for your precious life.

27 Can a man scoop fire into his lap, and his clothes not be burnt?

28 Or can one walk on hot coals, and his feet not be scorched?

29 So is he who goes in to his neighbor's wife. Whoever touches her will not be unpunished.

30 Men don't despise a thief, if he steals to satisfy himself when he is hungry:

31 but if he is found, he shall restore seven times. He shall give all the wealth of his house.

32 He who commits adultery with a woman is void of understanding. He who does it destroys his own soul.

33 He will get wounds and dishonor. His reproach will not be wiped away.

34 For jealousy arouses the fury of the husband. He won't spare in the

day of vengeance.

35 He won't regard any ransom, neither will he rest content, though you give many gifts.

Day 19 – Evening Sage Intake

Hebrews 8:10b – "I will put my laws into their mind, I will also write them on their heart. I will be their God, and they will be my people.

Proverbs 7

1 My son, keep my words. Lay up my commandments within you.

2 Keep my commandments and live! Guard my teaching as the apple of your eye.

3 Bind them on your fingers. Write them on the tablet of your heart.

4 Tell wisdom, "You are my sister." Call understanding your relative,

5 that they may keep you from the strange woman, from the foreigner who flatters with her words.

6 For at the window of my house, I looked out through my lattice.

7 I saw amongst the simple ones. I discerned amongst the youths a young man void of understanding,

8 passing through the street near her corner, he went the way to her house,

9 in the twilight, in the evening of the day, in the middle of the night and in the darkness.

10 Behold, there a woman met him with the attire of a prostitute, and with crafty intent.

11 She is loud and defiant. Her feet don't stay in her house.

12 Now she is in the streets, now in the squares, and lurking at every corner.

13 So she caught him, and kissed him. With an impudent face she said to him:

14 "Sacrifices of peace offerings are with me. Today I have paid my vows.

15 Therefore I came out to meet you, to diligently seek your face, and I have found you.

16 I have spread my couch with carpets of tapestry, with striped cloths of the yarn of Egypt.

17 I have perfumed my bed with myrrh, aloes, and cinnamon.

18 Come, let's take our fill of loving until the morning. Let's solace ourselves with loving.

19 For my husband isn't at home. He has gone on a long journey.

20 He has taken a bag of money with him. He will come home at the full moon."

21 With persuasive words, she led him astray. With the flattering of her lips, she seduced him.

22 He followed her immediately, as an ox goes to the slaughter, as a fool stepping into a noose.

23 Until an arrow strikes through his liver, as a bird hurries to the snare, and doesn't know that it will cost his life.

24 Now therefore, sons, listen to me. Pay attention to the words of my mouth.

25 Don't let your heart turn to her ways. Don't go astray in her paths,

26 for she has thrown down many wounded. Yes, all her slain are a mighty army.

27 Her house is the way to Sheol, going down to the rooms of death.

Day 20 – Morning Sage Intake

Jeremiah 29:13 – You shall seek me, and find me, when you shall search for me with all your heart.

Proverbs 8

1 Doesn't wisdom cry out? Doesn't understanding raise her voice?

2 On the top of high places by the way, where the paths meet, she stands.

3 Beside the gates, at the entry of the city, at the entry doors, she cries aloud:

4 "To you men, I call! I send my voice to the sons of mankind.

5 You simple, understand prudence. You fools, be of an understanding heart.

6 Hear, for I will speak excellent things. The opening of my lips is for right things.

7 For my mouth speaks truth. Wickedness is an abomination to my lips.

8 All the words of my mouth are in righteousness. There is nothing crooked or perverse in them.

9 They are all plain to him who understands, right to those who find knowledge.

10 Receive my instruction rather than silver; knowledge rather than choice gold.

11 For wisdom is better than rubies. All the things that may be desired can't be compared to it.

12 "I, wisdom, have made prudence my dwelling. Find out knowledge and discretion.

13 The fear of the LORD is to hate evil. I hate pride, arrogance, the evil way, and the perverse mouth.

14 Counsel and sound knowledge are mine. I have understanding and power.

15 By me kings reign, and princes decree justice.

16 By me princes rule; nobles, and all the righteous rulers of the earth.

17 I love those who love me. Those who seek me diligently will find me.

18 With me are riches, honor, enduring wealth, and prosperity.

19 My fruit is better than gold, yes, than fine gold; my yield than choice silver.

20 I walk in the way of righteousness, in the middle of the paths of justice;

21 That I may give wealth to those who love me. I fill their treasuries.

22 "The LORD possessed me in the beginning of his work, before his deeds of old.

23 I was set up from everlasting, from the beginning, before the earth existed.

24 When there were no depths, I was born, when there were no springs abounding with water.

25 Before the mountains were settled in place, before the hills, I was born;

26 while as yet he had not made the earth, nor the fields, nor the beginning of the dust of the world.

27 When he established the heavens, I was there; when he set a circle on the surface of the deep,

28 when he established the clouds above, when the springs of the deep became strong,

29 when he gave to the sea its boundary, that the waters should not

violate his commandment, when he marked out the foundations of the earth;

30 then I was the craftsman by his side. I was a delight day by day, always rejoicing before him,

31 Rejoicing in his whole world. My delight was with the sons of men.

32 "Now therefore, my sons, listen to me, for blessed are those who keep my ways.

33 Hear instruction, and be wise. Don't refuse it.

34 Blessed is the man who hears me, watching daily at my gates, waiting at my door posts.

35 For whoever finds me, finds life, and will obtain favor from the LORD.

36 But he who sins against me wrongs his own soul. All those who hate me love death."

Day 20 – Evening Sage Intake

God wants you to know, in the deepest part of you, that you can trust Him. This is one of the most important lessons that you will ever learn as you walk with Him.

Proverbs 9

1 Wisdom has built her house. She has carved out her seven pillars.

2 She has prepared her meat. She has mixed her wine. She has also set her table.

3 She has sent out her maidens. She cries from the highest places of the city:

4 "Whoever is simple, let him turn in here!" As for him who is void of understanding, she says to him,

5 "Come, eat some of my bread, drink some of the wine which I have mixed!

6 Leave your simple ways, and live. Walk in the way of understanding."

7 He who corrects a mocker invites insult. He who reproves a wicked man invites abuse.

8 Don't reprove a scoffer, lest he hate you. Reprove a wise man, and

he will love you.

9 Instruct a wise man, and he will be still wiser. Teach a righteous man, and he will increase in learning.

10 The fear of the LORD is the beginning of wisdom. The knowledge of the Holy One is understanding.

11 For by me your days will be multiplied. The years of your life will be increased.

12 If you are wise, you are wise for yourself. If you mock, you alone will bear it.

13 The foolish woman is loud, undisciplined, and knows nothing.

14 She sits at the door of her house, on a seat in the high places of the city,

15 to call to those who pass by, who go straight on their ways,

16 "Whoever is simple, let him turn in here." as for him who is void of understanding, she says to him,

17 "Stolen water is sweet. Food eaten in secret is pleasant."

18 But he doesn't know that the departed spirits are there, that her guests are in the depths of Sheol.

Day 21 – Morning Sage Intake

Verse 12 says that "love covers all wrongs". I think that is a great verse for you to spend some time considering today. How is your "life of love" going?

Proverbs 10

1 The proverbs of Solomon. A wise son makes a glad father; but a foolish son brings grief to his mother.

2 Treasures of wickedness profit nothing, but righteousness delivers from death.

3 The LORD will not allow the soul of the righteous to go hungry, but he thrusts away the desire of the wicked.

4 He becomes poor who works with a lazy hand, but the hand of the diligent brings wealth.

5 He who gathers in summer is a wise son, but he who sleeps during the harvest is a son who causes shame.

6 Blessings are on the head of the righteous, but violence covers the

mouth of the wicked.

7 The memory of the righteous is blessed, but the name of the wicked will rot.

8 The wise in heart accept commandments, but a chattering fool will fall.

9 He who walks blamelessly walks surely, but he who perverts his ways will be found out.

10 One winking with the eye causes sorrow, but a chattering fool will fall.

11 The mouth of the righteous is a spring of life, but violence covers the mouth of the wicked.

12 Hatred stirs up strife, but love covers all wrongs.

13 Wisdom is found on the lips of him who has discernment, but a rod is for the back of him who is void of understanding.

14 Wise men lay up knowledge, but the mouth of the foolish is near ruin.

15 The rich man's wealth is his strong city. The destruction of the poor is their poverty.

16 The labor of the righteous leads to life. The increase of the wicked leads to sin.

17 He is in the way of life who heeds correction, but he who forsakes reproof leads others astray.

18 He who hides hatred has lying lips. He who utters a slander is a fool.

19 In the multitude of words there is no lack of disobedience, but he who restrains his lips does wisely.

20 The tongue of the righteous is like choice silver. The heart of the wicked is of little worth.

21 The lips of the righteous feed many, but the foolish die for lack of understanding.

22 The LORD's blessing brings wealth, and he adds no trouble to it.

23 It is a fool's pleasure to do wickedness, but wisdom is a man of understanding's pleasure.

24 What the wicked fear, will overtake them, but the desire of the righteous will be granted.

25 When the whirlwind passes, the wicked is no more; but the righteous stand firm forever.

26 As vinegar to the teeth, and as smoke to the eyes, so is the sluggard to those who send him.

27 The fear of the LORD prolongs days, but the years of the wicked shall be shortened.

28 The prospect of the righteous is joy, but the hope of the wicked will perish.

29 The way of the LORD is a stronghold to the upright, but it is a destruction to the workers of iniquity.

30 The righteous will never be removed, but the wicked will not dwell in the land.

31 The mouth of the righteous produces wisdom, but the perverse tongue will be cut off.

32 The lips of the righteous know what is acceptable, but the mouth of the wicked is perverse.

Day 21 – Evening Sage Intake

You reap what you sow! Galatians 6:7-10 – Don't be deceived. God is not mocked, for whatever a man sows, that he will also reap. For he who sows to his own flesh will from the flesh reap corruption. But he who sows to the Spirit will from the Spirit reap eternal life. Let us not be weary in doing good, for we will reap in due season, if we don't give up. So then, as we have opportunity, let's do what is good towards all men, and especially towards those who are of the household of the faith.

Proverbs 11

1 A false balance is an abomination to the LORD, but accurate weights are his delight.

2 When pride comes, then comes shame, but with humility comes wisdom.

3 The integrity of the upright shall guide them, but the perverseness of the treacherous shall destroy them.

4 Riches don't profit in the day of wrath, but righteousness delivers from death.

5 The righteousness of the blameless will direct his way, but the wicked shall fall by his own wickedness.

6 The righteousness of the upright shall deliver them, but the unfaithful will be trapped by evil desires.

7 When a wicked man dies, hope perishes, and expectation of power comes to nothing.

8 A righteous person is delivered out of trouble, and the wicked takes his place.

9 With his mouth the godless man destroys his neighbor, but the righteous will be delivered through knowledge.

10 When it goes well with the righteous, the city rejoices. When the wicked perish, there is shouting.

11 By the blessing of the upright, the city is exalted, but it is overthrown by the mouth of the wicked.

12 One who despises his neighbor is void of wisdom, but a man of understanding holds his peace.

13 One who brings gossip betrays a confidence, but one who is of a trustworthy spirit is one who keeps a secret.

14 Where there is no wise guidance, the nation falls, but in the multitude of counselors there is victory.

15 He who is collateral for a stranger will suffer for it, but he who refuses pledges of collateral is secure.

16 A gracious woman obtains honor, but violent men obtain riches.

17 The merciful man does good to his own soul, but he who is cruel troubles his own flesh.

18 Wicked people earn deceitful wages, but one who sows righteousness reaps a sure reward.

19 He who is truly righteous gets life. He who pursues evil gets death.

20 Those who are perverse in heart are an abomination to the LORD, but those whose ways are blameless are his delight.

21 Most certainly, the evil man will not be unpunished, but the offspring of the righteous will be delivered.

22 Like a gold ring in a pig's snout, is a beautiful woman who lacks discretion.

23 The desire of the righteous is only good. The expectation of the wicked is wrath.

24 There is one who scatters, and increases yet more. There is one who withholds more than is appropriate, but gains poverty.

25 The liberal soul shall be made fat. He who waters shall be watered also himself.

26 People curse someone who withholds grain, but blessing will be on the head of him who sells it.

27 He who diligently seeks good seeks favor, but he who searches

after evil, it shall come to him.

28 He who trusts in his riches will fall, but the righteous shall flourish as the green leaf.

29 He who troubles his own house shall inherit the wind. The foolish shall be servant to the wise of heart.

30 The fruit of the righteous is a tree of life. He who is wise wins souls.

31 Behold, the righteous shall be repaid in the earth; how much more the wicked and the sinner!

Congratulations! This is the end of the third week. Usually, it takes about three weeks to make something a habit. Reading through the Proverbs on a regular basis will go a long way in helping your light shine for Jesus!

Day 22 – Morning Sage Intake

Verse 25 says, "Anxiety in a man's heart weighs it down, but a kind word makes it glad." We live in a grumpy world, filled with bad news and fear which is often spun and repeated over and over again to make it seem worse and more fearful. Make it a point today, to encourage at least two people with a kind word or action. God can use your acts of kindness to change people's hearts and lives forever!

Proverbs 12

1 Whoever loves correction loves knowledge, but he who hates reproof is stupid.

2 A good man shall obtain favor from the LORD, but he will condemn a man of wicked devices.

3 A man shall not be established by wickedness, but the root of the righteous shall not be moved.

4 A worthy woman is the crown of her husband, but a disgraceful wife is as rottenness in his bones.

5 The thoughts of the righteous are just, but the advice of the wicked is deceitful.

6 The words of the wicked are about lying in wait for blood, but the

speech of the upright rescues them.

7 The wicked are overthrown, and are no more, but the house of the righteous shall stand.

8 A man shall be commended according to his wisdom, but he who has a warped mind shall be despised.

9 Better is he who is lightly esteemed, and has a servant, than he who honors himself, and lacks bread.

10 A righteous man respects the life of his animal, but the tender mercies of the wicked are cruel.

11 He who tills his land shall have plenty of bread, but he who chases fantasies is void of understanding.

12 The wicked desires the plunder of evil men, but the root of the righteous flourishes.

13 An evil man is trapped by sinfulness of lips, but the righteous shall come out of trouble.

14 A man shall be satisfied with good by the fruit of his mouth. The work of a man's hands shall be rewarded to him.

15 The way of a fool is right in his own eyes, but he who is wise listens to counsel.

16 A fool shows his annoyance the same day, but one who overlooks an insult is prudent.

17 He who is truthful testifies honestly, but a false witness lies.

18 There is one who speaks rashly like the piercing of a sword, but the tongue of the wise heals.

19 Truth's lips will be established forever, but a lying tongue is only momentary.

20 Deceit is in the heart of those who plot evil, but joy comes to the promoters of peace.

21 No mischief shall happen to the righteous, but the wicked shall be filled with evil.

22 Lying lips are an abomination to the LORD, but those who do the truth are his delight.

23 A prudent man keeps his knowledge, but the hearts of fools proclaim foolishness.

24 The hands of the diligent ones shall rule, but laziness ends in slave labor.

25 Anxiety in a man's heart weighs it down, but a kind word makes it glad.

26 A righteous person is cautious in friendship, but the way of the

wicked leads them astray.

27 The slothful man doesn't roast his game, but the possessions of diligent men are prized.

28 In the way of righteousness is life; in its path there is no death.

Day 22 – Evening Sage Intake

Hope deferred makes the heart sick. Every hope deferred, every broken thing, every failure, should be a reminder that this temporary life will never be perfect, but, in His mercy and grace, Jesus has made a way for us to get back into the relationship we had with God before the fall. This is not as good as it gets and you don't need to make it your life's purpose to try and fix it. Instead, fix your eyes on Jesus, knowing that real now and forever life is experienced in Him!

Proverbs 13

1 A wise son listens to his father's instruction, but a scoffer doesn't listen to rebuke.

2 By the fruit of his lips, a man enjoys good things; but the unfaithful crave violence.

3 He who guards his mouth guards his soul. One who opens wide his lips comes to ruin.

4 The soul of the sluggard desires, and has nothing, but the desire of the diligent shall be fully satisfied.

5 A righteous man hates lies, but a wicked man brings shame and disgrace.

6 Righteousness guards the way of integrity, but wickedness overthrows the sinner.

7 There are some who pretend to be rich, yet have nothing. There are some who pretend to be poor, yet have great wealth.

8 The ransom of a man's life is his riches, but the poor hear no threats.

9 The light of the righteous shines brightly, but the lamp of the wicked is snuffed out.

10 Pride only breeds quarrels, but with ones who take advice is wisdom.

11 Wealth gained dishonestly dwindles away, but he who gathers by

hand makes it grow.

12 Hope deferred makes the heart sick, but when longing is fulfilled, it is a tree of life.

13 Whoever despises instruction will pay for it, but he who respects a command will be rewarded.

14 The teaching of the wise is a spring of life, to turn from the snares of death.

15 Good understanding wins favor; but the way of the unfaithful is hard.

16 Every prudent man acts from knowledge, but a fool exposes folly.

17 A wicked messenger falls into trouble, but a trustworthy envoy gains healing.

18 Poverty and shame come to him who refuses discipline, but he who heeds correction shall be honored.

19 Longing fulfilled is sweet to the soul, but fools detest turning from evil.

20 One who walks with wise men grows wise, but a companion of fools suffers harm.

21 Misfortune pursues sinners, but prosperity rewards the righteous.

22 A good man leaves an inheritance to his children's children, but the wealth of the sinner is stored for the righteous.

23 An abundance of food is in poor people's fields, but injustice sweeps it away.

24 One who spares the rod hates his son, but one who loves him is careful to discipline him.

25 The righteous one eats to the satisfying of his soul, but the belly of the wicked goes hungry.

Day 23 – Morning Sage Intake

Verse 30 says "The life of the body is a heart at peace, but envy rots the bones." Start off today by being thankful for at least five things. Being thankful for what you have instead of worrying about what you don't have, or envying what somebody else has, will set your heart at peace!

Proverbs 14

1 Every wise woman builds her house, but the foolish one tears it down with her own hands.

2 He who walks in his uprightness fears the LORD, but he who is perverse in his ways despises him.

3 The fool's talk brings a rod to his back, but the lips of the wise protect them.

4 Where no oxen are, the crib is clean, but much increase is by the strength of the ox.

5 A truthful witness will not lie, but a false witness pours out lies.

6 A scoffer seeks wisdom, and doesn't find it, but knowledge comes easily to a discerning person.

7 Stay away from a foolish man, for you won't find knowledge on his lips.

8 The wisdom of the prudent is to think about his way, but the folly of fools is deceit.

9 Fools mock at making atonement for sins, but amongst the upright there is good will.

10 The heart knows its own bitterness and joy; he will not share these with a stranger.

11 The house of the wicked will be overthrown, but the tent of the upright will flourish.

12 There is a way which seems right to a man, but in the end it leads to death.

13 Even in laughter the heart may be sorrowful, and mirth may end in heaviness.

14 The unfaithful will be repaid for his own ways; likewise a good man will be rewarded for his ways.

15 A simple man believes everything, but the prudent man carefully considers his ways.

16 A wise man fears, and shuns evil, but the fool is hot headed and reckless.

17 He who is quick to become angry will commit folly, and a crafty man is hated.

18 The simple inherit folly, but the prudent are crowned with knowledge.

19 The evil bow down before the good, and the wicked at the gates of the righteous.

20 The poor person is shunned even by his own neighbor, but the rich person has many friends.

21 He who despises his neighbor sins, but blessed is he who has pity on the poor.

22 Don't they go astray who plot evil? But love and faithfulness belong to those who plan good.

23 In all hard work there is profit, but the talk of the lips leads only to poverty.

24 The crown of the wise is their riches, but the folly of fools crowns them with folly.

25 A truthful witness saves souls, but a false witness is deceitful.

26 In the fear of the LORD is a secure fortress, and he will be a refuge for his children.

27 The fear of the LORD is a fountain of life, turning people from the snares of death.

28 In the multitude of people is the king's glory, but in the lack of people is the destruction of the prince.

29 He who is slow to anger has great understanding, but he who has a quick temper displays folly.

30 The life of the body is a heart at peace, but envy rots the bones.

31 He who oppresses the poor shows contempt for his Maker, but he who is kind to the needy honors him.

32 The wicked is brought down in his calamity, but in death, the righteous has a refuge.

33 Wisdom rests in the heart of one who has understanding, and is even made known in the inward part of fools.

34 Righteousness exalts a nation, but sin is a disgrace to any people.

35 The king's favor is towards a servant who deals wisely, but his wrath is towards one who causes shame.

Day 23 – Evening Sage Intake

I am so thankful that God hears our prayers. Think about how amazing that is. God, the creator of the universe, hears us when we pray. So, with that in mind, make sure you take time to pray everyday!

Proverbs 15

1 A gentle answer turns away wrath, but a harsh word stirs up anger.
2 The tongue of the wise commends knowledge, but the mouth of fools gush out folly.
3 The LORD's eyes are everywhere, keeping watch on the evil and the good.
4 A gentle tongue is a tree of life, but deceit in it crushes the spirit.
5 A fool despises his father's correction, but he who heeds reproof shows prudence.
6 In the house of the righteous is much treasure, but the income of the wicked brings trouble.
7 The lips of the wise spread knowledge; not so with the heart of fools.
8 The sacrifice made by the wicked is an abomination to the LORD, but the prayer of the upright is his delight.
9 The way of the wicked is an abomination to the LORD, but he loves him who follows after righteousness.
10 There is stern discipline for one who forsakes the way: whoever hates reproof shall die.
11 Sheol and Abaddon are before the LORD—how much more then the hearts of the children of men!
12 A scoffer doesn't love to be reproved; he will not go to the wise.
13 A glad heart makes a cheerful face; but an aching heart breaks the spirit.
14 The heart of one who has understanding seeks knowledge, but the mouths of fools feed on folly.
15 All the days of the afflicted are wretched, but one who has a cheerful heart enjoys a continual feast.
16 Better is little, with the fear of the LORD, than great treasure with trouble.
17 Better is a dinner of herbs, where love is, than a fattened calf with hatred.
18 A wrathful man stirs up contention, but one who is slow to anger appeases strife.
19 The way of the sluggard is like a thorn patch, but the path of the upright is a highway.
20 A wise son makes a father glad, but a foolish man despises his mother.

21 Folly is joy to one who is void of wisdom, but a man of understanding keeps his way straight.

22 Where there is no counsel, plans fail; but in a multitude of counselors they are established.

23 Joy comes to a man with the reply of his mouth. How good is a word at the right time!

24 The path of life leads upward for the wise, to keep him from going downward to Sheol.

25 The LORD will uproot the house of the proud, but he will keep the widow's borders intact.

26 The LORD detests the thoughts of the wicked, but the thoughts of the pure are pleasing.

27 He who is greedy for gain troubles his own house, but he who hates bribes will live.

28 The heart of the righteous weighs answers, but the mouth of the wicked gushes out evil.

29 The LORD is far from the wicked, but he hears the prayer of the righteous.

30 The light of the eyes rejoices the heart. Good news gives health to the bones.

31 The ear that listens to reproof lives, and will be at home amongst the wise.

32 He who refuses correction despises his own soul, but he who listens to reproof gets understanding.

33 The fear of the LORD teaches wisdom. Before honor is humility.

Day 24 – Morning Sage Intake

A blessed life comes from trusting in the Lord and obeying His Word as we live each day by trying to do the next right thing!

Proverbs 16

1 The plans of the heart belong to man, but the answer of the tongue is from the LORD.

2 All the ways of a man are clean in his own eyes; but the LORD weighs the motives.

3 Commit your deeds to the LORD, and your plans shall succeed.

4 The LORD has made everything for its own end—yes, even the wicked for the day of evil.

5 Everyone who is proud in heart is an abomination to the LORD: they shall certainly not be unpunished.

6 By mercy and truth iniquity is atoned for. By the fear of the LORD men depart from evil.

7 When a man's ways please the LORD, he makes even his enemies to be at peace with him.

8 Better is a little with righteousness, than great revenues with injustice.

9 A man's heart plans his course, but the LORD directs his steps.

10 Inspired judgements are on the lips of the king. He shall not betray his mouth.

11 Honest balances and scales are the LORD's; all the weights in the bag are his work.

12 It is an abomination for kings to do wrong, for the throne is established by righteousness.

13 Righteous lips are the delight of kings. They value one who speaks the truth.

14 The king's wrath is a messenger of death, but a wise man will pacify it.

15 In the light of the king's face is life. His favor is like a cloud of the spring rain.

16 How much better it is to get wisdom than gold! Yes, to get understanding is to be chosen rather than silver.

17 The highway of the upright is to depart from evil. He who keeps his way preserves his soul.

18 Pride goes before destruction, and a haughty spirit before a fall.

19 It is better to be of a lowly spirit with the poor, than to divide the plunder with the proud.

20 He who heeds the Word finds prosperity. Whoever trusts in the LORD is blessed.

21 The wise in heart shall be called prudent. Pleasantness of the lips promotes instruction.

22 Understanding is a fountain of life to one who has it, but the punishment of fools is their folly.

23 The heart of the wise instructs his mouth, and adds learning to his lips.

24 Pleasant words are a honeycomb, sweet to the soul, and health to

the bones.

25 There is a way which seems right to a man, but in the end it leads to death.

26 The appetite of the laboring man labors for him; for his mouth urges him on.

27 A worthless man devises mischief. His speech is like a scorching fire.

28 A perverse man stirs up strife. A whisperer separates close friends.

29 A man of violence entices his neighbor, and leads him in a way that is not good.

30 One who winks his eyes to plot perversities, one who compresses his lips, is bent on evil.

31 Grey hair is a crown of glory. It is attained by a life of righteousness.

32 One who is slow to anger is better than the mighty; one who rules his spirit, than he who takes a city.

33 The lot is cast into the lap, but its every decision is from the LORD.

Day 24 – Evening Sage Intake

What an amazing blessing grand children are! My grand children are definitely a "crown" to me, so I guess that makes me an old man! (See Verse 6)

Proverbs 17

1 Better is a dry morsel with quietness, than a house full of feasting with strife.

2 A servant who deals wisely will rule over a son who causes shame, and shall have a part in the inheritance amongst the brothers.

3 The refining pot is for silver, and the furnace for gold, but the LORD tests the hearts.

4 An evildoer heeds wicked lips. A liar gives ear to a mischievous tongue.

5 Whoever mocks the poor reproaches his Maker. He who is glad at calamity shall not be unpunished.

6 Children's children are the crown of old men; the glory of children

are their parents.

7 Arrogant speech isn't fitting for a fool, much less do lying lips fit a prince.

8 A bribe is a precious stone in the eyes of him who gives it; wherever he turns, he prospers.

9 He who covers an offense promotes love; but he who repeats a matter separates best friends.

10 A rebuke enters deeper into one who has understanding than a hundred lashes into a fool.

11 An evil man seeks only rebellion; therefore a cruel messenger shall be sent against him.

12 Let a bear robbed of her cubs meet a man, rather than a fool in his folly.

13 Whoever rewards evil for good, evil shall not depart from his house.

14 The beginning of strife is like breaching a dam, therefore stop contention before quarreling breaks out.

15 He who justifies the wicked, and he who condemns the righteous, both of them alike are an abomination to the LORD.

16 Why is there money in the hand of a fool to buy wisdom, since he has no understanding?

17 A friend loves at all times; and a brother is born for adversity.

18 A man void of understanding strikes hands, and becomes collateral in the presence of his neighbor.

19 He who loves disobedience loves strife. One who builds a high gate seeks destruction.

20 One who has a perverse heart doesn't find prosperity, and one who has a deceitful tongue falls into trouble.

21 He who becomes the father of a fool grieves. The father of a fool has no joy.

22 A cheerful heart makes good medicine, but a crushed spirit dries up the bones.

23 A wicked man receives a bribe in secret, to pervert the ways of justice.

24 Wisdom is before the face of one who has understanding, but the eyes of a fool wander to the ends of the earth.

25 A foolish son brings grief to his father, and bitterness to her who bore him.

26 Also to punish the righteous is not good, nor to flog officials for

their integrity.

27 He who spares his words has knowledge. He who is even tempered is a man of understanding.

28 Even a fool, when he keeps silent, is counted wise. When he shuts his lips, he is thought to be discerning.

Day 25 – Morning Sage Intake

Every time I read verse 22 I think about how thankful I am that God put my lovely wife Alice in my life. She is a constant reminder to me of the favor of the Lord!

Proverbs 18

1 An unfriendly man pursues selfishness, and defies all sound judgement.

2 A fool has no delight in understanding, but only in revealing his own opinion.

3 When wickedness comes, contempt also comes, and with shame comes disgrace.

4 The words of a man's mouth are like deep waters. The fountain of wisdom is like a flowing brook.

5 To be partial to the faces of the wicked is not good, nor to deprive the innocent of justice.

6 A fool's lips come into strife, and his mouth invites beatings.

7 A fool's mouth is his destruction, and his lips are a snare to his soul.

8 The words of a gossip are like dainty morsels: they go down into a person's innermost parts.

9 One who is slack in his work is brother to him who is a master of destruction.

10 The LORD's name is a strong tower: the righteous run to him, and are safe.

11 The rich man's wealth is his strong city, like an unscalable wall in his own imagination.

12 Before destruction the heart of man is proud, but before honor is humility.

13 He who gives answer before he hears, that is folly and shame to him.

14 A man's spirit will sustain him in sickness, but a crushed spirit, who can bear?

15 The heart of the discerning gets knowledge. The ear of the wise seeks knowledge.

16 A man's gift makes room for him, and brings him before great men.

17 He who pleads his cause first seems right; until another comes and questions him.

18 The lot settles disputes, and keeps strong ones apart.

19 A brother offended is more difficult than a fortified city; and disputes are like the bars of a fortress.

20 A man's stomach is filled with the fruit of his mouth. With the harvest of his lips he is satisfied.

21 Death and life are in the power of the tongue; those who love it will eat its fruit.

22 Whoever finds a wife finds a good thing, and obtains favor of the LORD.

23 The poor plead for mercy, but the rich answer harshly.

24 A man of many companions may be ruined, but there is a friend who sticks closer than a brother.

Day 25 – Evening Sage Intake

John 15:12 – "This is my commandment, that you love one another, even as I have loved you.

Proverbs 19

1 Better is the poor who walks in his integrity than he who is perverse in his lips and is a fool.

2 It isn't good to have zeal without knowledge; nor being hasty with one's feet and missing the way.

3 The foolishness of man subverts his way; his heart rages against the LORD.

4 Wealth adds many friends, but the poor is separated from his friend.

5 A false witness shall not be unpunished. He who pours out lies shall not go free.

6 Many will entreat the favor of a ruler, and everyone is a friend to a

man who gives gifts.

7 All the relatives of the poor shun him: how much more do his friends avoid him! He pursues them with pleas, but they are gone.

8 He who gets wisdom loves his own soul. He who keeps understanding shall find good.

9 A false witness shall not be unpunished. He who utters lies shall perish.

10 Delicate living is not appropriate for a fool, much less for a servant to have rule over princes.

11 The discretion of a man makes him slow to anger. It is his glory to overlook an offense.

12 The king's wrath is like the roaring of a lion, but his favor is like dew on the grass.

13 A foolish son is the calamity of his father. A wife's quarrels are a continual dripping.

14 House and riches are an inheritance from fathers, but a prudent wife is from the LORD.

15 Slothfulness casts into a deep sleep. The idle soul shall suffer hunger.

16 He who keeps the commandment keeps his soul, but he who is contemptuous in his ways shall die.

17 He who has pity on the poor lends to the LORD; he will reward him.

18 Discipline your son, for there is hope; don't be a willing party to his death.

19 A hot-tempered man must pay the penalty, for if you rescue him, you must do it again.

20 Listen to counsel and receive instruction, that you may be wise in your latter end.

21 There are many plans in a man's heart, but the LORD's counsel will prevail.

22 That which makes a man to be desired is his kindness. A poor man is better than a liar.

23 The fear of the LORD leads to life, then contentment; he rests and will not be touched by trouble.

24 The sluggard buries his hand in the dish; he will not so much as bring it to his mouth again.

25 Flog a scoffer, and the simple will learn prudence; rebuke one who has understanding, and he will gain knowledge.

26 He who robs his father and drives away his mother, is a son who causes shame and brings reproach.

27 If you stop listening to instruction, my son, you will stray from the words of knowledge.

28 A corrupt witness mocks justice, and the mouth of the wicked gulps down iniquity.

29 Penalties are prepared for scoffers, and beatings for the backs of fools.

Day 26 – Morning Sage Intake

Verse 9 is a reminder of how amazing it is that God sees us "in Christ". Once we are saved by confessing with our mouths that Jesus is Lord and believing in our hearts that God raised Him from the dead, our sins are forgiven and gone. God no longer sees us in the mess we have made of our lives, but He sees us in the perfection of His Son. That is "Good News"!

Proverbs 20

1 Wine is a mocker, and beer is a brawler. Whoever is led astray by them is not wise.

2 The terror of a king is like the roaring of a lion. He who provokes him to anger forfeits his own life.

3 It is an honor for a man to keep aloof from strife; but every fool will be quarreling.

4 The sluggard will not plow by reason of the winter; therefore he shall beg in harvest, and have nothing.

5 Counsel in the heart of man is like deep water; but a man of understanding will draw it out.

6 Many men claim to be men of unfailing love, but who can find a faithful man?

7 A righteous man walks in integrity. Blessed are his children after him.

8 A king who sits on the throne of judgement scatters away all evil with his eyes.

9 Who can say, "I have made my heart pure. I am clean and without sin?"

10 Differing weights and differing measures, both of them alike are an abomination to the LORD.

11 Even a child makes himself known by his doings, whether his work is pure, and whether it is right.

12 The hearing ear, and the seeing eye, the LORD has made even both of them.

13 Don't love sleep, lest you come to poverty. Open your eyes, and you shall be satisfied with bread.

14 "It's no good, it's no good," says the buyer; but when he is gone his way, then he boasts.

15 There is gold and abundance of rubies; but the lips of knowledge are a rare jewel.

16 Take the garment of one who puts up collateral for a stranger; and hold him in pledge for a wayward woman.

17 Fraudulent food is sweet to a man, but afterwards his mouth is filled with gravel.

18 Plans are established by advice; by wise guidance you wage war!

19 He who goes about as a tale-bearer reveals secrets; therefore don't keep company with him who opens wide his lips.

20 Whoever curses his father or his mother, his lamp shall be put out in blackness of darkness.

21 An inheritance quickly gained at the beginning, won't be blessed in the end.

22 Don't say, "I will pay back evil." Wait for the LORD, and he will save you.

23 The LORD detests differing weights, and dishonest scales are not pleasing.

24 A man's steps are from the LORD; how then can man understand his way?

25 It is a snare to a man to make a rash dedication, then later to consider his vows.

26 A wise king winnows out the wicked, and drives the threshing wheel over them.

27 The spirit of man is the LORD's lamp, searching all his innermost parts.

28 Love and faithfulness keep the king safe. His throne is sustained by love.

29 The glory of young men is their strength. The splendor of old men is their grey hair.

30 Wounding blows cleanse away evil, and beatings purge the innermost parts.

Day 26 – Evening Sage Intake

Verse 23 – "Whoever guards his mouth and his tongue keeps his soul from troubles." Can I get a witness!

Proverbs 21

1 The king's heart is in the LORD's hand like the watercourses. He turns it wherever he desires.
2 Every way of a man is right in his own eyes, but the LORD weighs the hearts.
3 To do righteousness and justice is more acceptable to the LORD than sacrifice.
4 A high look, and a proud heart, the lamp of the wicked, is sin.
5 The plans of the diligent surely lead to profit; and everyone who is hasty surely rushes to poverty.
6 Getting treasures by a lying tongue is a fleeting vapor for those who seek death.
7 The violence of the wicked will drive them away, because they refuse to do what is right.
8 The way of the guilty is devious, but the conduct of the innocent is upright.
9 It is better to dwell in the corner of the housetop, than to share a house with a contentious woman.
10 The soul of the wicked desires evil; his neighbor finds no mercy in his eyes.
11 When the mocker is punished, the simple gains wisdom. When the wise is instructed, he receives knowledge.
12 The Righteous One considers the house of the wicked, and brings the wicked to ruin.
13 Whoever stops his ears at the cry of the poor, he will also cry out, but shall not be heard.
14 A gift in secret pacifies anger; and a bribe in the cloak, strong wrath.
15 It is joy to the righteous to do justice; but it is a destruction to the

workers of iniquity.

16 The man who wanders out of the way of understanding shall rest in the assembly of the departed spirits.

17 He who loves pleasure shall be a poor man. He who loves wine and oil shall not be rich.

18 The wicked is a ransom for the righteous; the treacherous for the upright.

19 It is better to dwell in a desert land, than with a contentious and fretful woman.

20 There is precious treasure and oil in the dwelling of the wise; but a foolish man swallows it up.

21 He who follows after righteousness and kindness finds life, righteousness, and honor.

22 A wise man scales the city of the mighty, and brings down the strength of its confidence.

23 Whoever guards his mouth and his tongue keeps his soul from troubles.

24 The proud and haughty man, "scoffer" is his name; he works in the arrogance of pride.

25 The desire of the sluggard kills him, for his hands refuse to labor.

26 There are those who covet greedily all day long; but the righteous give and don't withhold.

27 The sacrifice of the wicked is an abomination: how much more, when he brings it with a wicked mind!

28 A false witness will perish, and a man who listens speaks to eternity.

29 A wicked man hardens his face; but as for the upright, he establishes his ways.

30 There is no wisdom nor understanding nor counsel against the LORD.

31 The horse is prepared for the day of battle; but victory is with the LORD.

"Whoever guards his mouth and his tongue keeps his soul from troubles."

Day 27 – Morning Sage Intake

The first part of verse 9 says, "He who has a generous eye will be blessed". We need to ask God to help us to see like He sees. Don't let the people you encounter during your day simply fade into the scenery and machinery of your life. Look for ways to encourage at least two people everyday. When you encourage two people, three people are encouraged because God will encourage you!

Proverbs 22

1 A good name is more desirable than great riches, and enjoying favor is better than silver and gold.

2 The rich and the poor have this in common: The LORD is the maker of them all.

3 A prudent man sees danger, and hides himself; but the simple pass on, and suffer for it.

4 The result of humility and the fear of the LORD is wealth, honor, and life.

5 Thorns and snares are in the path of the wicked: whoever guards his soul stays from them.

6 Train up a child in the way he should go, and when he is old he will not depart from it.

7 The rich rule over the poor. The borrower is servant to the lender.

8 He who sows wickedness reaps trouble, and the rod of his fury will be destroyed.

9 He who has a generous eye will be blessed; for he shares his food with the poor.

10 Drive out the mocker, and strife will go out; yes, quarrels and insults will stop.

11 He who loves purity of heart and speaks gracefully is the king's friend.

12 The LORD's eyes watch over knowledge; but he frustrates the words of the unfaithful.

13 The sluggard says, "There is a lion outside! I will be killed in the streets!"

14 The mouth of an adulteress is a deep pit: he who is under the LORD's wrath will fall into it.

15 Folly is bound up in the heart of a child: the rod of discipline drives it far from him.

16 Whoever oppresses the poor for his own increase and whoever gives to the rich, both come to poverty.

17 Turn your ear, and listen to the words of the wise. Apply your heart to my teaching.

18 For it is a pleasant thing if you keep them within you, if all of them are ready on your lips.

19 That your trust may be in the LORD, I teach you today, even you.

20 Haven't I written to you thirty excellent things of counsel and knowledge,

21 To teach you truth, reliable words, to give sound answers to the ones who sent you?

22 Don't exploit the poor, because he is poor; and don't crush the needy in court;

23 for the LORD will plead their case, and plunder the life of those who plunder them.

24 Don't befriend a hot-tempered man, and don't associate with one who harbors anger:

25 lest you learn his ways, and ensnare your soul.

26 Don't you be one of those who strike hands, of those who are collateral for debts.

27 If you don't have means to pay, why should he take away your bed from under you?

28 Don't move the ancient boundary stone, which your fathers have set up.

29 Do you see a man skilled in his work? He will serve kings. He won't serve obscure men.

Day 27 – Evening Sage Intake

The second part of verse 24 says, "Whoever fathers a wise child delights in him". Sarah and Douglas, you are indeed a delight to me!

Proverbs 23

1 When you sit to eat with a ruler, consider diligently what is before you;

2 put a knife to your throat, if you are a man given to appetite.

3 Don't be desirous of his dainties, since they are deceitful food.

4 Don't weary yourself to be rich. In your wisdom, show restraint.

5 Why do you set your eyes on that which is not? For it certainly sprouts wings like an eagle and flies in the sky.

6 Don't eat the food of him who has a stingy eye, and don't crave his delicacies:

7 for as he thinks about the cost, so he is. "Eat and drink!" he says to you, but his heart is not with you.

8 The morsel which you have eaten you shall vomit up, and lose your good words.

9 Don't speak in the ears of a fool, for he will despise the wisdom of your words.

10 Don't move the ancient boundary stone. Don't encroach on the fields of the fatherless:

11 for their Defender is strong. He will plead their case against you.

12 Apply your heart to instruction, and your ears to the words of knowledge.

13 Don't withhold correction from a child. If you punish him with the rod, he will not die.

14 Punish him with the rod, and save his soul from Sheol.

15 My son, if your heart is wise, then my heart will be glad, even mine:

16 yes, my heart will rejoice, when your lips speak what is right.

17 Don't let your heart envy sinners; but rather fear the LORD all the day long.

18 Indeed surely there is a future hope, and your hope will not be cut off.

19 Listen, my son, and be wise, and keep your heart on the right path!

20 Don't be amongst ones drinking too much wine, or those who gorge themselves on meat:

21 for the drunkard and the glutton shall become poor; and drowsiness clothes them in rags.

22 Listen to your father who gave you life, and don't despise your mother when she is old.

23 Buy the truth, and don't sell it. Get wisdom, discipline, and understanding.

24 The father of the righteous has great joy. Whoever fathers a wise child delights in him.

25 Let your father and your mother be glad! Let her who bore you rejoice!

26 My son, give me your heart; and let your eyes keep in my ways.

27 For a prostitute is a deep pit; and a wayward wife is a narrow well.

28 Yes, she lies in wait like a robber, and increases the unfaithful amongst men.

29 Who has woe? Who has sorrow? Who has strife? Who has complaints? Who has needless bruises? Who has bloodshot eyes?

30 Those who stay long at the wine; those who go to seek out mixed wine.

31 Don't look at the wine when it is red, when it sparkles in the cup, when it goes down smoothly.

32 In the end, it bites like a snake, and poisons like a viper.

33 Your eyes will see strange things, and your mind will imagine confusing things.

34 Yes, you will be as he who lies down in the middle of the sea, or as he who lies on top of the rigging:

35 "They hit me, and I was not hurt! They beat me, and I don't feel it! When will I wake up? I can do it again. I can find another."

Day 28 – Morning Sage Intake

Ephesians 4:15 – "but speaking truth in love, we may grow up in all things into him, who is the head, Christ."

Proverbs 24

1 Don't be envious of evil men; neither desire to be with them:

2 for their hearts plot violence, and their lips talk about mischief.

3 Through wisdom a house is built; by understanding it is established;

4 by knowledge the rooms are filled with all rare and beautiful treasure.

5 A wise man has great power; and a knowledgeable man increases strength;

6 for by wise guidance you wage your war; and victory is in many advisers.

7 Wisdom is too high for a fool: he doesn't open his mouth in the gate.

8 One who plots to do evil will be called a schemer.

9 The schemes of folly are sin. The mocker is detested by men.

10 If you falter in the time of trouble, your strength is small.

11 Rescue those who are being led away to death! Indeed, hold back those who are staggering to the slaughter!

12 If you say, "Behold, we didn't know this"; doesn't he who weighs the hearts consider it? He who keeps your soul, doesn't he know it? Shall he not render to every man according to his work?

13 My son, eat honey, for it is good; the droppings of the honeycomb, which are sweet to your taste:

14 so you shall know wisdom to be to your soul; if you have found it, then there will be a reward, your hope will not be cut off.

15 Don't lay in wait, wicked man, against the habitation of the righteous. Don't destroy his resting place:

16 for a righteous man falls seven times, and rises up again; but the wicked are overthrown by calamity.

17 Don't rejoice when your enemy falls. Don't let your heart be glad when he is overthrown;

18 lest the LORD see it, and it displease him, and he turn away his wrath from him.

19 Don't fret yourself because of evildoers; neither be envious of the wicked:

20 for there will be no reward to the evil man; and the lamp of the wicked shall be snuffed out.

21 My son, fear the LORD and the king. Don't join those who are rebellious:

22 for their calamity will rise suddenly; the destruction from them both—who knows?

23 These also are sayings of the wise. To show partiality in judgement is not good.

24 He who says to the wicked, "You are righteous"; peoples shall curse him, and nations shall abhor him—

25 but it will go well with those who convict the guilty, and a rich blessing will come on them.

26 An honest answer is like a kiss on the lips.

27 Prepare your work outside, and get your fields ready. Afterwards, build your house.

28 Don't be a witness against your neighbor without cause. Don't deceive with your lips.

29 Don't say, "I will do to him as he has done to me; I will render to the man according to his work."

30 I went by the field of the sluggard, by the vineyard of the man void of understanding;

31 Behold, it was all grown over with thorns. Its surface was covered with nettles, and its stone wall was broken down.

32 Then I saw, and considered well. I saw, and received instruction:

33 a little sleep, a little slumber, a little folding of the hands to sleep;

34 so your poverty will come as a robber, and your want as an armed man.

Day 28 – Evening Sage Intake

I like that the Apostle Paul gives advice from the Proverbs. He quotes from verses 21-22 in this great advice for living found in the Book of Romans! Romans 12:18-21 – "If it is possible, as much as it is up to you, be at peace with all men. Don't seek revenge yourselves, beloved, but give place to God's wrath. For it is written, "Vengeance belongs to me; I will repay, says the Lord." Therefore "If your enemy is hungry, feed him. If he is thirsty, give him a drink; for in doing so, you will heap coals of fire on his head." Don't be overcome by evil, but overcome evil with good.

Proverbs 25

1 These also are proverbs of Solomon, which the men of Hezekiah king of Judah copied out.

2 It is the glory of God to conceal a thing, but the glory of kings is to search out a matter.

3 As the heavens for height, and the earth for depth, so the hearts of kings are unsearchable.

4 Take away the dross from the silver, and material comes out for the refiner;

5 Take away the wicked from the king's presence, and his throne will be established in righteousness.

6 Don't exalt yourself in the presence of the king, or claim a place amongst great men;

7 for it is better that it be said to you, "Come up here," than that you

should be put lower in the presence of the prince, whom your eyes have seen.

8 Don't be hasty in bringing charges to court. What will you do in the end when your neighbor shames you?

9 Debate your case with your neighbor, and don't betray the confidence of another;

10 lest one who hears it put you to shame, and your bad reputation never depart.

11 A word fitly spoken is like apples of gold in settings of silver.

12 As an earring of gold, and an ornament of fine gold, so is a wise man's rebuke to an obedient ear.

13 As the cold of snow in the time of harvest, so is a faithful messenger to those who send him; for he refreshes the soul of his masters.

14 As clouds and wind without rain, so is he who boasts of gifts deceptively.

15 By patience a ruler is persuaded. A soft tongue breaks the bone.

16 Have you found honey? Eat as much as is sufficient for you, lest you eat too much, and vomit it.

17 Let your foot be seldom in your neighbor's house, lest he be weary of you, and hate you.

18 A man who gives false testimony against his neighbor is like a club, a sword, or a sharp arrow.

19 Confidence in someone unfaithful in time of trouble is like a bad tooth, or a lame foot.

20 As one who takes away a garment in cold weather, or vinegar on soda, so is one who sings songs to a heavy heart.

21 If your enemy is hungry, give him food to eat. If he is thirsty, give him water to drink:

22 for you will heap coals of fire on his head, and the LORD will reward you.

23 The north wind produces rain: so a backbiting tongue brings an angry face.

24 It is better to dwell in the corner of the housetop, than to share a house with a contentious woman.

25 Like cold water to a thirsty soul, so is good news from a far country.

26 Like a muddied spring, and a polluted well, so is a righteous man who gives way before the wicked.

27 It is not good to eat much honey; nor is it honorable to seek one's own honor.

28 Like a city that is broken down and without walls is a man whose spirit is without restraint.

Day 29 – Morning Sage Intake

Verse 11 reminds me of Albert Einstein's definition of insanity: doing the same thing over and over again and expecting different results.

Proverbs 26

1 Like snow in summer, and as rain in harvest, so honor is not fitting for a fool.

2 Like a fluttering sparrow, like a darting swallow, so the undeserved curse doesn't come to rest.

3 A whip is for the horse, a bridle for the donkey, and a rod for the back of fools!

4 Don't answer a fool according to his folly, lest you also be like him.

5 Answer a fool according to his folly, lest he be wise in his own eyes.

6 One who sends a message by the hand of a fool is cutting off his own feet and drinking violence.

7 Like the legs of the lame that hang loose: so is a parable in the mouth of fools.

8 As one who binds a stone in a sling, so is he who gives honor to a fool.

9 Like a thorn bush that goes into the hand of a drunkard, so is a parable in the mouth of fools.

10 As an archer who wounds all, so is he who hires a fool or he who hires those who pass by.

11 As a dog that returns to his vomit, so is a fool who repeats his folly.

12 Do you see a man wise in his own eyes? There is more hope for a fool than for him.

13 The sluggard says, "There is a lion in the road! A fierce lion roams the streets!"

14 As the door turns on its hinges, so does the sluggard on his bed.

15 The sluggard buries his hand in the dish. He is too lazy to bring it back to his mouth.

16 The sluggard is wiser in his own eyes than seven men who answer with discretion.

17 Like one who grabs a dog's ears is one who passes by and meddles in a quarrel not his own.

18 Like a madman who shoots torches, arrows, and death,

19 is the man who deceives his neighbor and says, "Am I not joking?"

20 For lack of wood a fire goes out. Without gossip, a quarrel dies down.

21 As coals are to hot embers, and wood to fire, so is a contentious man to kindling strife.

22 The words of a whisperer are as dainty morsels, they go down into the innermost parts.

23 Like silver dross on an earthen vessel are the lips of a fervent one with an evil heart.

24 A malicious man disguises himself with his lips, but he harbors evil in his heart.

25 When his speech is charming, don't believe him; for there are seven abominations in his heart.

26 His malice may be concealed by deception, but his wickedness will be exposed in the assembly.

27 Whoever digs a pit shall fall into it. Whoever rolls a stone, it will come back on him.

28 A lying tongue hates those it hurts; and a flattering mouth works ruin.

Day 29 – Evening Sage Intake

I would encourage you to take a few moments and consider verse 19 – "Like water reflects a face, so a man's heart reflects the man". How is your reflection?

Proverbs 27

1 Don't boast about tomorrow; for you don't know what a day may bring.

2 Let another man praise you, and not your own mouth; a stranger,

and not your own lips.

3 A stone is heavy, and sand is a burden; but a fool's provocation is heavier than both.

4 Wrath is cruel, and anger is overwhelming; but who is able to stand before jealousy?

5 Better is open rebuke than hidden love.

6 Faithful are the wounds of a friend; although the kisses of an enemy are profuse.

7 A full soul loathes a honeycomb; but to a hungry soul, every bitter thing is sweet.

8 As a bird that wanders from her nest, so is a man who wanders from his home.

9 Perfume and incense bring joy to the heart; so does earnest counsel from a man's friend.

10 Don't forsake your friend and your father's friend. Don't go to your brother's house in the day of your disaster: better is a neighbor who is near than a distant brother.

11 Be wise, my son, and bring joy to my heart, then I can answer my tormentor.

12 A prudent man sees danger and takes refuge; but the simple pass on, and suffer for it.

13 Take his garment when he puts up collateral for a stranger. Hold it for a wayward woman!

14 He who blesses his neighbor with a loud voice early in the morning, it will be taken as a curse by him.

15 A continual dropping on a rainy day and a contentious wife are alike:

16 restraining her is like restraining the wind, or like grasping oil in his right hand.

17 Iron sharpens iron; so a man sharpens his friend's countenance.

18 Whoever tends the fig tree shall eat its fruit. He who looks after his master shall be honored.

19 Like water reflects a face, so a man's heart reflects the man.

20 Sheol and Abaddon are never satisfied; and a man's eyes are never satisfied.

21 The crucible is for silver, and the furnace for gold; but man is refined by his praise.

22 Though you grind a fool in a mortar with a pestle along with grain, yet his foolishness will not be removed from him.

23 Know well the state of your flocks, and pay attention to your herds:

24 for riches are not forever, nor does even the crown endure to all generations.

25 The hay is removed, and the new growth appears, the grasses of the hills are gathered in.

26 The lambs are for your clothing, and the goats are the price of a field.

27 There will be plenty of goats' milk for your food, for your family's food, and for the nourishment of your servant girls.

Day 30 – Morning Sage Intake

When we choose to do our own thing, we often find ourselves filled with worry and anxiety. When we choose to do the next right thing, we can rest in the peace and presence of God.

Proverbs 28

1 The wicked flee when no one pursues; but the righteous are as bold as a lion.

2 In rebellion, a land has many rulers, but order is maintained by a man of understanding and knowledge.

3 A needy man who oppresses the poor is like a driving rain which leaves no crops.

4 Those who forsake the law praise the wicked; but those who keep the law contend with them.

5 Evil men don't understand justice; but those who seek the LORD understand it fully.

6 Better is the poor who walks in his integrity, than he who is perverse in his ways, and he is rich.

7 Whoever keeps the law is a wise son; but he who is a companion of gluttons shames his father.

8 He who increases his wealth by excessive interest gathers it for one who has pity on the poor.

9 He who turns away his ear from hearing the law, even his prayer is an abomination.

10 Whoever causes the upright to go astray in an evil way, he will fall

into his own trap; but the blameless will inherit good.

11 The rich man is wise in his own eyes; but the poor who has understanding sees through him.

12 When the righteous triumph, there is great glory; but when the wicked rise, men hide themselves.

13 He who conceals his sins doesn't prosper, but whoever confesses and renounces them finds mercy.

14 Blessed is the man who always fears; but one who hardens his heart falls into trouble.

15 As a roaring lion or a charging bear, so is a wicked ruler over helpless people.

16 A tyrannical ruler lacks judgement. One who hates ill-gotten gain will have long days.

17 A man who is tormented by life blood will be a fugitive until death; no one will support him.

18 Whoever walks blamelessly is kept safe; but one with perverse ways will fall suddenly.

19 One who works his land will have an abundance of food; but one who chases fantasies will have his fill of poverty.

20 A faithful man is rich with blessings; but one who is eager to be rich will not go unpunished.

21 To show partiality is not good; yet a man will do wrong for a piece of bread.

22 A stingy man hurries after riches, and doesn't know that poverty waits for him.

23 One who rebukes a man will afterward find more favor than one who flatters with the tongue.

24 Whoever robs his father or his mother, and says, "It's not wrong." He is a partner with a destroyer.

25 One who is greedy stirs up strife; but one who trusts in the LORD will prosper.

26 One who trusts in himself is a fool; but one who walks in wisdom is kept safe.

27 One who gives to the poor has no lack; but one who closes his eyes will have many curses.

28 When the wicked rise, men hide themselves; but when they perish, the righteous thrive.

Day 30 – Evening Sage Intake

Ephesians 4:26-27 - "Be angry, and don't sin." Don't let the sun go down on your wrath, and don't give place to the evil one.

Proverbs 29

1 He who is often rebuked and stiffens his neck will be destroyed suddenly, with no remedy.

2 When the righteous thrive, the people rejoice; but when the wicked rule, the people groan.

3 Whoever loves wisdom brings joy to his father; but a companion of prostitutes squanders his wealth.

4 The king by justice makes the land stable, but he who takes bribes tears it down.

5 A man who flatters his neighbor spreads a net for his feet.

6 An evil man is snared by his sin, but the righteous can sing and be glad.

7 The righteous care about justice for the poor. The wicked aren't concerned about knowledge.

8 Mockers stir up a city, but wise men turn away anger.

9 If a wise man goes to court with a foolish man, the fool rages or scoffs, and there is no peace.

10 The bloodthirsty hate a man of integrity; and they seek the life of the upright.

11 A fool vents all of his anger, but a wise man brings himself under control.

12 If a ruler listens to lies, all of his officials are wicked.

13 The poor man and the oppressor have this in common: The LORD gives sight to the eyes of both.

14 The king who fairly judges the poor, his throne shall be established forever.

15 The rod of correction gives wisdom, but a child left to himself causes shame to his mother.

16 When the wicked increase, sin increases; but the righteous will see their downfall.

17 Correct your son, and he will give you peace; yes, he will bring delight to your soul.

18 Where there is no revelation, the people cast off restraint; but one who keeps the law is blessed.

19 A servant can't be corrected by words. Though he understands, yet he will not respond.

20 Do you see a man who is hasty in his words? There is more hope for a fool than for him.

21 He who pampers his servant from youth will have him become a son in the end.

22 An angry man stirs up strife, and a wrathful man abounds in sin.

23 A man's pride brings him low, but one of lowly spirit gains honor.

24 Whoever is an accomplice of a thief is an enemy of his own soul. He takes an oath, but dares not testify.

25 The fear of man proves to be a snare, but whoever puts his trust in the LORD is kept safe.

26 Many seek the ruler's favor, but a man's justice comes from the LORD.

27 A dishonest man detests the righteous, and the upright in their ways detest the wicked.

Day 31 – Morning Sage Intake

The first part of verse 5 says that "Every word of God is flawless". Paul expands that thought in 2 Timothy 3:16-17 – Every Scripture is God-breathed and profitable for teaching, for reproof, for correction, and for instruction in righteousness, that the man of God may be complete, thoroughly equipped for every good work.

Proverbs 30

1 The words of Agur the son of Jakeh, the revelation: the man says to Ithiel, to Ithiel and Ucal:

2 "Surely I am the most ignorant man, and don't have a man's understanding.

3 I have not learned wisdom, neither do I have the knowledge of the Holy One.

4 Who has ascended up into heaven, and descended? Who has gathered the wind in his fists? Who has bound the waters in his garment? Who has established all the ends of the earth? What is his

name, and what is his son's name, if you know?

5 "Every word of God is flawless. He is a shield to those who take refuge in him.

6 Don't you add to his words, lest he reprove you, and you be found a liar.

7 "Two things I have asked of you; don't deny me before I die:

8 remove far from me falsehood and lies. Give me neither poverty nor riches. Feed me with the food that is needful for me;

9 lest I be full, deny you, and say, 'Who is the LORD?' or lest I be poor, and steal, and so dishonor the name of my God.

10 "Don't slander a servant to his master, lest he curse you, and you be held guilty.

11 There is a generation that curses their father, and doesn't bless their mother.

12 There is a generation that is pure in their own eyes, yet are not washed from their filthiness.

13 There is a generation, oh how lofty are their eyes! Their eyelids are lifted up.

14 There is a generation whose teeth are like swords, and their jaws like knives, to devour the poor from the earth, and the needy from amongst men.

15 "The leach has two daughters: 'Give, give.' "There are three things that are never satisfied; four that don't say, 'Enough:'

16 Sheol, the barren womb; the earth that is not satisfied with water; and the fire that doesn't say, 'Enough.'

17 "The eye that mocks at his father, and scorns obedience to his mother: the ravens of the valley shall pick it out, the young eagles shall eat it.

18 "There are three things which are too amazing for me, four which I don't understand:

19 the way of an eagle in the air; the way of a serpent on a rock; the way of a ship in the middle of the sea; and the way of a man with a maiden.

20 "So is the way of an adulterous woman: she eats and wipes her mouth, and says, 'I have done nothing wrong.'

21 "For three things the earth tremble, and under four, it can't bear up:

22 for a servant when he is king; a fool when he is filled with food;

23 for an unloved woman when she is married; and a servant who is

heir to her mistress.

24 "There are four things which are little on the earth, but they are exceedingly wise:

25 the ants are not a strong people, yet they provide their food in the summer.

26 The conies are but a feeble folk, yet they make their houses in the rocks.

27 The locusts have no king, yet they advance in ranks.

28 You can catch a lizard with your hands, yet it is in kings' palaces.

29 "There are three things which are stately in their march, four which are stately in going:

30 the lion, which is mightiest amongst animals, and doesn't turn away for any;

31 the greyhound, the male goat also; and the king against whom there is no rising up.

32 "If you have done foolishly in lifting up yourself, or if you have thought evil, put your hand over your mouth.

33 For as the churning of milk produces butter, and the wringing of the nose produces blood; so the forcing of wrath produces strife."

Day 31 – Evening Sage Intake

Proverbs 31 contains amazing advice for living by doing the next right thing. The advice was given by a loving mother to her son to help him experience a full life. Thanks to moms everywhere for loving your children well! And a special thanks to my Mom as well. I love you!

Proverbs 31

1 The words of king Lemuel; the revelation which his mother taught him.

2 "Oh, my son! Oh, son of my womb! Oh, son of my vows!

3 Don't give your strength to women, nor your ways to that which destroys kings.

4 It is not for kings, Lemuel; it is not for kings to drink wine; nor for princes to say, 'Where is strong drink?'

5 Lest they drink, and forget the law, and pervert the justice due to

anyone who is afflicted.

6 Give strong drink to him who is ready to perish; and wine to the bitter in soul:

7 Let him drink, and forget his poverty, and remember his misery no more.

8 Open your mouth for the mute, in the cause of all who are left desolate.

9 Open your mouth, judge righteously, and serve justice to the poor and needy."

10 Who can find a worthy woman? For her price is far above rubies.

11 The heart of her husband trusts in her. He shall have no lack of gain.

12 She does him good, and not harm, all the days of her life.

13 She seeks wool and flax, and works eagerly with her hands.

14 She is like the merchant ships. She brings her bread from afar.

15 She rises also while it is yet night, gives food to her household, and portions for her servant girls.

16 She considers a field, and buys it. With the fruit of her hands, she plants a vineyard.

17 She arms her waist with strength, and makes her arms strong.

18 She perceives that her merchandise is profitable. Her lamp doesn't go out by night.

19 She lays her hands to the distaff, and her hands hold the spindle.

20 She opens her arms to the poor; yes, she extends her hands to the needy.

21 She is not afraid of the snow for her household; for all her household are clothed with scarlet.

22 She makes for herself carpets of tapestry. Her clothing is fine linen and purple.

23 Her husband is respected in the gates, when he sits amongst the elders of the land.

24 She makes linen garments and sells them, and delivers sashes to the merchant.

25 Strength and dignity are her clothing. She laughs at the time to come.

26 She opens her mouth with wisdom. Faithful instruction is on her tongue.

27 She looks well to the ways of her household, and doesn't eat the bread of idleness.

28 Her children rise up and call her blessed. Her husband also praises her:

29 "Many women do noble things, but you excel them all."

30 Charm is deceitful, and beauty is vain; but a woman who fears the LORD, she shall be praised.

31 Give her of the fruit of her hands! Let her works praise her in the gates!

Congratulations! You have read the entire book of Proverbs twice in 31 days. The wisdom contained in the Proverbs will help you to live by doing the next right thing and keep you shining bright in a very dark world. I would encourage you to keep up with your readings in the "Daily Sage Intake" and the "Daily Psalt Intake" each month. Next up we will be adding readings in the Old and New Testament and a devotional to help develop our disciple's hearts. Look for "Daily Bread Intake" and "Daily Cardio Training" online at:

www.spiritualfervor.com

Psalt and Sage Daily!